MW00784284

OUT OF BISAMBERG

Christiane Zehl Romero

Copyright © 2023 Christiane Zehl Romero

All rights reserved.

No part of this book may be reproduced, stored in a retrieval system, or transmitted, in any form or by any means, electronic, mechanical, photocopying, recording, or otherwise, without prior written permission from the publisher, except for brief quotations embodied in critical reviews and certain other noncommercial uses permitted by copyright law.

Contents

Introduction

Memories are unreliable, as we all know, and as I am often reminded when I share recollections with others who sometimes contradict what is certain and vivid in my mind. Yet, we cannot live, think, and love without our memories. We rely on them to understand ourselves and our world and to connect to those who have gone before us. Only if we remember them, they and the events and places they inhabited live on to provide the roots and the continuity human beings need.

Thus, despite the caveats, the following memoir will look back upon my childhood and youth as truthfully as I can, hoping to pass on to my American grandchildren where their roots on their father's side lie and what it was like for me to grow up in times and a culture so different from theirs. Who was the family they come from, who were the friends, teachers, and experiences that shaped me and, to a small degree, them? I hope that at some point later, they will be interested in an authentic report which I can provide now that I have reached a certain age and realize how little I knew and how many questions I should have asked but did not.

Much has been written by historians and memorialists about the years in which I grew up – the late 1930s to the late 1950s – because they were especially traumatic and difficult for Germany and my home country Austria. They included the Nazi-period with the holocaust and World War II, as well as their aftermath, the Cold War, events which demanded explanations but defied understanding. Many of my generation and the next tried to orient themselves by writing individual memoirs blaming their parents and grandparents for what they did and did not do. Without making excuses, I cannot and will not join them because I feel there is a gulf between my own experiences and such accounts. Although I have read much – history, memoirs, and literary texts – I still find it

1

frightening to try to fathom what happened on a large scale but also difficult to relate it to my own remembrances. Nevertheless, the following will attempt to see the people whom I loved and whom I lived with in the light of my own fragmented memories. I am grateful that I was spared their difficult choices but realize more and more clearly that my comfortable existence contained challenges which I did not consider and which I failed. My generation, including myself, will be blamed for the damage we did to our human and natural environment and rightly so. Still, if we hope to carry on with life on earth, we must know what came before us and bridge the gap between History and our individual stories by understanding our connections and our responsibilities. We need to have roots to grow, and as conscious human beings we need to know about them. All this sounds grand but the following memoir is intentionally low-key and undramatic.

Out of Bisamberg

I am a first-generation immigrant to the United States. But I've never thought of myself as an immigrant. I have double citizenship, US and Austrian, and even though I will probably die and be buried in the US, I feel more as a long-term visitor.

Like others who did not flee persecution or economic hardship, I am an "in-betweener," not fully at home anywhere but, thanks to modern transportation and my profession as a German literature and film teacher, able to go back and forth physically and intellectually. Although I have lived in the US for more than 50 years and studied English since childhood, I still have a slight accent that appears to be getting stronger as I grow older. Thus, people sometimes ask me where I come from. "From Vienna," I say proudly and expect the usual response, "Oh, what a beautiful city, I've been there!" or "I want to visit!" However, both, my answer and my pride, are somewhat misleading as well as misplaced.

Contemporary Map of Vienna and Surroundings

What I mean will hopefully become clear as I go along. What will also become clear, and what I realize as I look back, is how few questions I asked growing up and how little I reflected on what went on around me.

Beginnings

Yes, I was born in Vienna, in Floridsdorf, a working-class and now an immigrant district on the "other" side of the Danube, which for many proper Viennese, is the wrong side. Floridsdorf was only incorporated into the city in 1905 and became a major site for the social democratic resistance in its doomed fight against Austria's paramilitary Heimwehr during the "Civil War" of 1934. I mention this (although it has nothing to do with my mother's decision three years later to give birth in Floridsdorf) because as long as I lived in Austria and went to school there, this history was neither taught nor discussed. However, it shaped the coming years and the post-war period I grew up in. Some of the battle sites were within easy walking distance of my school.

Now, ironically, this history will be my last scholarly endeavor. I have worked on the German writer, Anna Seghers, for many years and, because of my Austrian background, have been asked to prepare the critical edition of Anna Seghers' novel about the Civil War of 1934, *Der Weg durch den Februar*.

In 1937, my mother may not even have been aware of these events. She lived in the nearby village of Bisamberg and had no connection to Floridsdorf other than knowing that the hospital there was the nearest and the best. Considering herself a "modern" woman, she did not want a home birth with a country midwife. Age may have also played a role; she was thirty-one when she had me, her first child, and at that time might have considered this age a risk factor. She had waited a long time to marry my father, whom she had known since they both were quite young. However, in those days, you did not wed until the husband was in a position to support his family. She had chosen my father over other suitors who had more to offer materially. However, the two I know about were country boys, my father was not. He had more education and different expectations, in addition to boyish good looks. So. she was prepared to be patient and wait.

Father as a young man

My Mother

Times were hard in Austria when my parents were young, in the so-called "Zwischenkriegszeit," the period between World War I and World War II. My father's telegram announcing his appointment as officer in the Austrian army is among the few carefully sorted papers my mother left me. Otherwise, what I say here about my mother's choices is speculation. I never asked her, and she did not usually talk about these things. I think she must have told me about her suitors, or perhaps somebody else did. They still lived in the village when I was growing up and I fully agreed with her selecting my father.

Wedding of Anna Zauninger and Richard Zehl

I also know that I was born during grape harvest; "Weinlese," we called it. My mother's father was a vintner, and the beginning of October was a crucial and intense period. Nobody had time to attend to her and me; another reason we were better off in a hospital. My father, it seems, was away on training exercises. Hospital stays after a birth were longer then (and still are in Austria), so the grapes were pressed, and the juice was in barrels when my mother brought me home to Bisamberg where my parents had rented a small apartment right across from my grandparents' house.

Proud parents

My father and mother were not going to stay there for long, though. They had plans to move out of rural Bisamberg and into the city of Vienna as soon as they could find an appropriate apartment there, which wasn't, and had not been, easy for at least a century. Indeed, my parents had many plans taking them out of the countryside and into the urban upper middle-class lifestyle they envisioned for themselves. But none of them materialized, at least not in the long run. Yet they never complained. They may have felt that they had forfeited the right to do so and, like so many of their and older generations, they were not prone to complaining.

"Anschluss"

I was little more than half a year old in 1938 when Hitler and his troops marched into Austria and were jubilantly received along their way to Vienna. Hitler, of course, did not march; he was driven in one of those cars that suggested power and elegance and enhanced his image, which to my perception from hindsight, badly needed all the props he used. Were my parents among the enthusiastic crowds? I don't think so. But it wasn't something we ever discussed. Nobody did in the Austria where I grew up, and certainly not in school or among the people I knew. Still, I assume that my parents were not the kind of people to stand by the side of the road to wave or to go to the Heldenplatz in Vienna to greet Hitler with "Sieg Heil" as he stood on the balcony of the Imperial Castle before jubilant masses. Of course, after the War, hardly anybody admitted to having been there.

On the other hand, however, I am sure that my parents did not oppose the "Anschluss." It promised them a brighter future than the little Austria, which had brought hunger, unemployment, and an authoritarian, strictly Catholic government. One of the few things my mother did tell me was that after World War I, hunger was worse than after World War II, even in the countryside. She was about twelve and watched carefully that her older sister did not get more of the scarce and dusty bread than she did. For my father and his family, the situation was acerbated since they were Lutheran and thus belonged to a very small, de facto second-class minority in Austria. They would be part of a major, in some regions the major, religious group in Germany.

Ironically, with respect to my initial remarks, during the Third Reich and for nine years after Bisamberg was part of Vienna, "Groß Wien," as the Nazis called it, after the "Anschluss." "Anschluss" means connection, but not really annexation, which is the term used in English. Under Hitler, Austria again became the "Ostmark" (Eastern March), referring to the early Middle Ages when a march was a border region dedicated to defending the Holy Roman Empire against invaders from the East. However, in the Third Reich, it was not meant as a defense so much as a stronghold for conquest in the East. As number three in the intermittent succession of empires, the

Holy Roman and the Wilhelminian being the first two, the Third Reich was supposed to be larger and last a thousand years longer than these two. For the "Ostmark," it turned out to be no more than seven. Only then, did all dreams of an Austrian connection, an "Anschluss," to Germany, dissolve. After the collapse of the Habsburg Empire (at the end of World War I), many had entertained that dream. But at that time, its realization had been forbidden by the allies.

However, like so many others in Austria, my parents had never wondered where the longed-for "Anschluss" would lead. One of the few questions I dared ask my father when I was an adult and had finally learned about the holocaust (nobody had talked or taught about it when I grew up), was if he had known about it. He said, "No." A Jewish colleague and friend whom I told of this response categorically declared, "I do not believe him. That is what everybody says." I did believe my father then, and I still do, but the line between what my parents knew and what they didn't is blurry. Surely, they must have been aware that the Jewish population of Vienna was being ostracized and driven away, and there is no indication that they ever protested such treatment. The Nazi propaganda they were being fed (and probably believed) spoke of the evil that Jews had brought to German and Austrian society. Nobody talked about the atrocities that were being committed against them. Something I read later in Peter Weiss' play *Die Ermittlung* [The Investigation] impressed me very deeply and has stayed with me even today: "If you do not object right away when something strikes you as wrong, you not only get used to it but also to things becoming worse."

My parents and others probably became used to small indignities and injustices against Jews, and then insensitive to larger ones. But what did they even see and hear? My father was not at home enough to experience firsthand what was happening in and around Vienna and had no Jewish friends, nor did my mother. I think neither of them knew any Jews. Still, they must have noticed that Vienna's

10

Jewish population, which had been sizeable and prominent, was disappearing. They probably paid little attention, perhaps even approved, of what was happening.

The environment in which both my parents grew up was not friendly to Jews to begin with. I think they shared the popular belief, embraced by Lutherans and Catholics alike, that Jews in Austria and especially in Vienna had become too wealthy and powerful. Also, Vienna housed many poor Jews who had come in steady streams from the East to flee the pogroms there, which made matters worse because these new arrivals appeared strange and unattractive, supporting the racial prejudices which were being propagated. They were frequently conflated with the rich, cultured, and assimilated Jews, who, themselves, looked down upon these poorer, more orthodox groups.

I remember my surprise and shock about a Jewish exile writer whom I was writing about and who expressed his resentment that upon his immigration to the US, there was no longer any distinction made between himself, the cultured man, and others with whom he felt he had nothing in common. As to my parents, I must admit to myself that they were antisemites, certainly before and during the Third Reich, even if they did not participate in any of the excesses against Jews, which were particularly egregious in Austria. Most likely, they never saw any, either.

Did their attitudes change after the War? They never said. Like many Austrians, they kept their mouths shut. The subject of Vienna's and Austria's Jews was never discussed when I grew up, not in my family and not in school. In Austria, it took much longer than in Germany (into the nineties) for the country to squarely face its past and its responsibility for what had happened, and it, at best, had let happen.

Personally, I never consciously met Jews until I came to the US and never really read or thought about their fate while growing up. In the post-war period, much of the reading all around me was still subtly and not so subtly antisemitic and racist. Only when my younger brother inherited our parents' house, did he decide to cleanse our large bookcase from what he considered "Nazi-infected" writing. We had still grown up with it.

Right after the War, my parents, like many others, struggled to prove that they had not been members of the Nazi party, but that did not account for where their sympathies had lain. And they worked hard to establish themselves yet one more time. By then, they had three children to take care of. My youngest brother was born in 1947. Like so many, they did not wish to look back; the present struggle was enough. I know my father became a member of post-war Austria's Social Democratic Party. He would not vote for the right-wing Volkspartei [People's Party] affiliated with the Catholic Church, nor did he want to support the FPÖ [Free Party of Austria], which consisted mostly of former Nazis and, later, Neo Nazis.

The Vienna Apartment

For a short period during the War, it looked like my parents were on their way to fulfilling their dreams. Back then, we lived in downtown Vienna, in what I remember as a large apartment on Berggasse, in the 9th district, not too far from the house that Sigmund Freud was forced to vacate. I am sure my parents knew nothing about him or his expulsion. Even when I was a student in the late 1950s, Freud was not talked about much in Austria. His house on Berggasse was not marked, and every day when I went to the English-American Institute at the University, I walked past his undistinguished-looking bust in a row of totally forgotten doctors in the arcades. At that time, I knew very little about who he was, but enough to wonder why he was not accorded more prominence.

What my parents might have known, though, was the possible fact that the previous owners of the apartment that was finally assigned to them were Jews who had been forced to leave, and quite likely under more terrible circumstances and with a worse destination than Freud. Again, I am speculating because nothing was ever said, not at the time nor later when I could and should have asked. For many years I only regretted the loss of that apartment, a place I remembered vividly in its early 1940s splendor.

The ninth district was where successful Jews had moved from the second, which is right across a waterway called the *Donaukanal*. Before the first "regulation" of the many rivers and rivulets which made up the Danube and frequently flooded the surrounding area, this had been *the* Danube that ran through the center of the city. As I read, many wealthy Jews from the ninth were driven away much earlier than their poorer brethren across the *Donaukanal*, who had fewer or no means of getting out in time.

However, when we moved into our apartment, it was already 1943, with the "Final Solution" in full force. Thus, I ask myself now if the previous, presumably Jewish, owners had been able to leave in time and if there were other tenants before us, or if the original occupants had stayed on until their forced removal. Nowadays, many of the Viennese houses, from which Jews were deported, have small brass plaques inserted into the sidewalks next to the entrance doors to remember names and dates. They exist in many European countries and are called "Stolpersteine" [Stumblingstones] in German. There are none by "our" door. When my older brother and I visited the house some years ago, we found offices of the Austrian police's sex crimes division in our former apartment. Perhaps they didn't want any plaques, or perhaps the restaurant on the ground floor, which has been there since we were children, refused them.

I was not even six when we moved into the apartment, yet I was already quite sensitive to my physical surroundings. I had no understanding, though, of what was going on around me in the larger society. At home, in my school, and everywhere else I went, Jews and their fate was not spoken of, as if they did not even exist and never had. Despite that, one memory stayed with me throughout the years and suggests that I did have a vague sense about something not being right.

It was a comment made when we showed the new apartment – to family, I assume – about black burn marks on the parquet floor around one of the stoves that heated the place. Ostensibly, it was a derogatory aside on the previous inhabitants' housekeeping, but I did not forget it. It was quite distinct. Even though the significance of this memory has only occurred to me much later, there must have been a reason for my unease beyond bad housekeeping, a reason I have forgotten. Perhaps it was a racist slur. Of course, my current assumption that the apartment had belonged to Jews, may be wrong altogether, I have no certainty, but it is very likely, and I may have picked up vibes that I could not place. In my experience, feelings associated with an event linger much longer in memory than facts.

At that time, I also saw yellow stars without knowing what they meant. This occurred when we walked to my aunt's house in the Second District. My mother's older sister, who was also my godmother, lived there. This district is called *Leopoldstadt*, ironically named after an emperor who was anything but good to his Jewish subjects.

When we walked to my aunt's, we always took a shortcut that led us through dark and gloomy back streets where we encountered few passersby; among them were the only people I ever saw who wore the yellow star. Although we went past them quickly, and the stars were never very conspicuous, the encounters were disturbing to me.

As much as I try, I cannot recall the response I received when I asked, but I know I did ask. The answer must have been of the noncommittal sort that adults give to children when they want to stop their questions. However, my mother appeared to take these yellow stars and the people who wore them for granted, and none of the adults around me ever mentioned them. Still, I recall that they struck me as ominous – why? Perhaps because they were rare and

14

unusual to me and/or because of the sad and furtive aura around the people who wore them, in combination with the empty and dreary-looking streets which were their backdrop. As a young child, and probably not unusually so, I had an especially fine sense for social ostracisms and exclusions of all kinds and was torn between the horrors of "contamination" and deep sympathy.

Mother Annerl and sister Mitzi

My aunt, Tante Mitzi, had married into a family which originally came from Germany but had been living in the *Leopoldstadt* district for a long time. They ran a large business there, selling hardware, including the lucrative supplies needed for boats, in one part and household items and fine china in the other. These were separate stores; one was supervised by my aunt, the other by my uncle and his father. Like many in the district, the family was not Jewish; on the contrary, the men were German nationalists and happy about the "Anschluss." My uncle was even a Nazi, something I only found out recently. I assume his father, an imposing gentleman, was the same. I do not believe my aunt was, at least not an official Party

15

Member. They all lived in the large apartment house above the stores.

Another couple, poorer relatives of that family but good friends of my mother's, also had an apartment on the same floor. We visited them as well and I remember frequent conversations about their daughter, who was a teenager then but had already chosen to become a "Diakonissin," a type of protestant nun, somewhere in Germany. I only met her after the War when she had left her order, returned to Vienna, and married a doctor with whom she lived in a huge apartment in one of the *Jugendstil* houses along the *Wienzeile*, where my mother and I once visited them. By then, I was a little disappointed in her. From an early age, I had heard praises about her, her beauty, her intelligence, and her dedication to nursing, a profession she had chosen herself. Everybody in the family admired her for it. To me, she was a distant, unreachable, and fascinating star when I was a little girl and remained one when I was a teenager and finally met her. However, it bothered me that she had given up her order and profession so readily.

After the War, her parents lived in one of the many small castles strewn all over Lower Austria. This castle was deserted, except for its outbuildings, where these friends had created an apartment for themselves and where we visited them. Our hosts showed us around in the castle though. There were long hallways with room after room, each with an antechamber where the maid or manservant would sleep. These were all guestrooms for when the place was in use, during summers.

I did not hear what eventually happened to this castle but know that many of the others are still being maintained by municipal governments and used for festivals and exhibitions, or by private owners such as well-to-do artists or writers. It always surprises me how many there are. Eventually, I lost track of these friends, but I do not think my parents did, although that happened with others to whom they had been close in their youth. In the immediate postwar period, people tried to connect, but life then drew them apart for good.

When we were five or six, I enjoyed our visits to my aunt's, despite the long walk from our apartment to and through the *Leopoldstadt*. I loved seeing our cousin Harry, who was a High School student back then, and performed magic tricks for us. In early 1945, he was killed on the southeastern outskirts of Vienna, the second of the two sons my aunt lost in World War II. His older brother, whom I do not remember ever seeing, was already "missing in action" on the Russian front. That is what it still says on the family grave. My aunt refused to have him declared dead.

She had only those two children and desperately tried to save Harry, the younger, who was drafted at the last minute to "defend Vienna." The story I heard was that my aunt went to his quarters to beg him to come home; the War would soon be over, and she could hide him. He refused because he felt he could not leave his comrades, and promptly "fell" (the euphemism used for those who died in action.)

Recently, I read about the motivation that made him stay and got him killed, which was very common among soldiers who kept fighting the losing battles, like the Germans at the end of the War. It was loyalty to their comrades, not their leaders or "the fatherland," which moved them. I had really admired this handsome, fun-loving cousin and still see him in front of me, making my gloves disappear and reappear.

Cousin Harry

My aunt's apartment was traditionally furnished and comfortable. As a student, I spent quite a few nights there, especially when I was late with a paper and did not want to take the time to go back to Bisamberg – a frequent occurrence throughout my academic career. I could pull an all-nighter in my cousins' former room, which was kept as if they would return. In the late morning, my aunt always came up from her office to have her "Gabelfrühstück" [second breakfast], which she shared with me. She was kind and friendly, yet I always had the feeling that she was no longer there – as in not really interested in her life. She conducted it conscientiously and dutifully, but with her children gone, it had lost all luster, and nothing was important anymore. I was sorry for her but always enjoyed visiting and liked her no-nonsense comments and her quiet apartment.

As a little girl, though, I much preferred ours. My fondest memories are of the gaily decorated children's room with facing Murphy beds and a large table in between for games – we never played on the floor as my children in the US did – a birthday party in the large dining room, it must have been my sixth, the bookcase in the "Herrenzimmer" [gentlemen's room] – there was no "salon" – and my mother's "Psyche" in the bedroom, a low dressing table with large moveable mirrors and a little stool in front. It was what a lady had to have at the time. Although my mother never liked makeup, she did use the mirrors whenever she made a dress for herself or me. You could see yourself from all sides. We also had a maid's room, which we did not need, and used as a "Rumpelkammer" [junkroom]. Later, when I read about the seduction of maids by their young masters, I pictured that room. Looking back, I realize that our apartment represented the progressive tastes of the time, with preferences for clean, simple lines, light-colored wood, and geometrically patterned textiles. I loved the furnishings and the spaciousness of it all and never had that again until I was well into adulthood.

While we were living there, my brother and I were sent to play with other children in the park along the *Donaukanal*. It was just a few steps from our house across a major street, which nowadays is much too busy to allow small children to cross on their own. At the time, there was little traffic, and my mother had no problem letting us go out by ourselves. She was by no means unusual in that respect and gave us typical warnings about not going with strangers. Such warnings did not help us in one instance which stayed with me, although it turned out to be okay: A couple came to our little group of playmates looking for a child small enough to squeeze through

19

the bars of a window next to their apartment door, a common set-up in older houses. The couple said they had forgotten their keys inside and wanted us to come along to see who would fit through the bars and retrieve them. I was wary but did not dare to oppose adults. We all followed to a dark and foreboding hallway where they picked one of us; thank goodness neither my brother nor me.

The chosen child scrambled inside as the rest of us stayed and watched. Nothing bad happened, and we all received chocolates as a reward for helping. I do not think we told our mother about this little adventure, though. In general, I must say that most things in Vienna, except for our apartment, struck me as gloomy and a bit scary, including my school and my classroom. The explanations I give myself now are the dearth of sunshine in late fall and winter when we were there and the lack of trees in between the tall greyish apartment buildings.

One event meant to cheer us up happened right across the street from our house in the daunting red brick complex of the *Rossau Barracks* – now there is a building in between. These barracks were built under Emperor Francis Joseph after he had ordered Vienna's ramparts and walls razed in 1857. The famous *Ringstraße*, a wide tree-lined boulevard, was built on the land that became available. It showcases representative buildings in different historical styles, from the pseudo-gothic *Votivkirche* to Austria's most important theater, the *Burgtheater*, to the town hall, the Parliament, the Opera, and many impressive apartment houses.

The *Ringstraße* was not only meant to be grand though, it also had to be very wide for a practical political purpose, namely to prevent any chance of protesters erecting barricades, impeding the movement of police and soldiers as had happened in the narrow streets of the inner city during the revolution of 1848. For further protection, barracks had to be built at strategic points to keep troops ready, in case the lower classes from the outer districts of Vienna would rise again. Some of the barracks, most prominently this one, still stand. It now houses the Austrian Ministry of Defense and was lately renamed "Amtsgebäude" [Office Building] *Rossau Bernardis-Schmid*, after two resisters of the Nazis. During my childhood, it was occupied by the German *Wehrmacht* [armed forces]. However, back then, there was no chance of an uprising by Viennese of any class.

Usually, we children kept a respectful distance from the soldiers and activities far across the street, but this time, we were invited inside for carousel and horseback riding. The occasion was probably a so-called "Tag der Wehrmacht" [Day of the Armed Forces] or another similar propaganda event. In the autumn of 1943, after the fall of Stalingrad, the German army apparently still found the time and the horses for such events. I admired horseback riding, probably because of photographs I had of my father in his army uniform on a horse, even jumping, and long into adulthood, I wanted to learn to ride. However, despite repeated attempts, I never did because it turned out that I was afraid of horses, which the animals sensed. They threw me repeatedly until I gave up. Perhaps "riding" in the *Rossau* barracks amid all the noise and commotion and being led around by men in uniforms lay at the source of my fears. I certainly did not enjoy the event and would never overcome my skittishness with horses.

Soldier Father

My father visited us once in the apartment, the only leave I recall, although there must have been more, certainly at the beginning of the war. He had been a professional soldier in the Austrian army since 1936, and along with his fellow officers, he was integrated into the *Wehrmacht,* when Hitler annexed Austria. Thus, he was absent for most of my earlier childhood. During the visit, I remember, I loved, sitting on the rim of the bathtub, watching him shave. I was fascinated by the foam he beat up in a little basin and by the other manly utensils, especially the knife-like razor blade that he sharpened on a strap before using. Except for my grandfather,

21

who had a handlebar mustache and no bathroom – he went to the barber for a shave – I was not used to having a man around.

My father was in his early thirties then and good-looking according to Nazi ideals; tall, blond, and blue-eyed. His looks and his commanding presence, besides his administrative skills, of course, may have helped him rise steeply in his career as a soldier, even though he never was a member of the Nazi Party. At least that is what he later asserted, and what I believe.

However, as I said, he was not an opponent of the regime either, certainly not at the beginning. Whether and when he changed his mind, I do not know, and he never said. My interpretation of his original attitude is infused by my limited knowledge of his family's tradition, which, even if it was not military, was always government service. My reading over the years also tells me that besides his basic sympathies for the "Anschluss," he, like many in the officer corps, thought of himself as a professional soldier and member of the military who had held prestigious and privileged positions in German and Austrian society for centuries. Although somewhat diminished by World War I, this general attitude determined their self-perception and made many of them believe that they were beyond politics.

Soldier Father

My father was a member of the General Staff and in charge of supplies, but never in the hinterland, always on the front, first in the West, then the East. I have no idea, though, from where I have that knowledge, but I do.

Klaus and Me Enjoying our Father

Father with his Staff in Crimea

At one point, I did research in the Historical Archives of the Austrian Army about somebody else. The person I saw asked me about my father and told me that his last rank had been that of a "Generalleutnant" [Lieutenant General]; until then, I had thought it was Major. This man offered me research on my father, but at the time, I refused. My father was no longer alive, so I could not talk to him in person, even if I mustered the courage to ask him detailed questions. And without that possibility, it felt like sneaking behind his back – then. Now I regret my reticence.

On the Russian front, my father came close enough to the actual fighting, but as best I know, he did not participate in it. I imagine that towards the end of the War, supplying the troops must have been a nightmare of a job. Yet, later he never talked about these experiences. All we had was a box of photographs which he must have sent home over the years. In one, he stood with his staff, all well dressed and well nourished, in front of a newly built blockhouse in Crimea. In another, he is on horseback. I loved looking at those photographs when I was about ten or eleven, but I never sat down with my father to talk about them. I remember only two things he mentioned casually in some unrelated context. One was about house plants and their odor-absorbing qualities, which he and his staff learned to appreciate after they had thrown them out of the houses where they moved. I do not recall the words he used, but "occupy" was not among them, nor did it occur to me to ask about the original inhabitants and if they had been thrown out as well. The other remark concerned his driver, who had raced him to the Baltic just in time to catch one of the last ships going west. There were no details, though, and for a long time, I naïvely thought that they had driven all the way from Crimea. It turned out that the German army had already retreated to the Baltic and that it was just a question of making it to a ship. I wonder what happened to his staff; there were too many of them to fit into a single car.

The photographs are gone as well as the bundles of letters that my father had written over the years. My mother cleaned most of that out when she emptied our attic and decided what she would leave for me/us. It was very little. What she did want us to have, were ten letters and cards my father wrote at the War's end. They are marked "Feldpost" [mail from the field], which during the Third Reich had priority and was faithfully transmitted very late into the War. Mail from home to the front was less reliable. In his notes, my father complains that the latest news he had from my mother was from January, while his letters, the ones I have, are dated from February 10 to March 16, 1945. They all come from East Prussia. He wrote frequently, mostly prepared cards and one-page letters on specially designed "Feldpost" paper, plus two longer regular letters. One of these recalls my parents' ninth wedding anniversary and speaks of his love, which he says is greater than ever. The "Feldpost" cards and one-page notes, all carry the imprint: "Es gibt in diesem

Schicksalskampf / Für uns nur ein Gebot: / Wer ehrenhaft kämpft, kann damit / das Leben für sich und seine Lieben retten. / Der Führer" [There is only one commandment for this fateful battle: By fighting honorably, you can save your own and your loved ones' lives.] The slogan does not make sense to me now, and I doubt it made any then. In addition, the cards also carry the descriptors and injunctions: "TAPFER UND TREU" [valiant and loyal].

My father's own messages repeat themselves as well but are basic and personal: He is well, no need to worry about him. He admonishes my mother to be "tapfer" – the word has infested everybody, albeit with different meanings – and to remain cheerful. Everything will "somehow" turn out fine; he will make it home, and they will have many more happy years together. Only one time does he refer to the need to "speak seriously." He then implies that he might not see my mother again, reminds her of his bank account number, and tells her that their life together has been wonderful, even though they have not been together all that much. They have used every minute well and loved each other deeply. He appreciates her more than ever, is grateful to her, and is sure of her love for him. I wish that later, when I was a teenager, and my father was often impatient with himself and, by extension, with my mother, he would have read those letters. I am sure, though, that she never forgot about them, and, ultimately, he did not either. Everyday life and war-related asthma just wore him down.

In his last notes from the front, which he admits surrounds them on three sides and is very close, my father is more concerned about my mother and us, the children, than about himself. News about the bombing raids over Germany and Austria was no secret; on the contrary, it was relayed to the troops and served as propaganda to keep fighting spirits up. He also worries whether there is enough for us to eat and wishes he could send some of the abundance available to him and his men. He mentions that they eat everything they find in the villages where they are being quartered and jokingly complains that among all the food the population has canned and preserved, there is not enough fruit. Is he talking about the food left behind by the German population that fled, or were they taking it away from the people who stayed behind? The only complaint he has, besides comments on the weather and the thaws which cause mud everywhere, is lodging. It is becoming very cramped, no more newly built blockhouses. At one point, he reports that he and his men all sleep together in one room, no larger than the kitchen in Bisamberg. At another time, he speaks of the many refugees and that he has two women with four children in his quarters. Implied in his remarks but never foregrounded is the fact that they are on the run, are encircled, and have nowhere to go but into the Baltic. The only place name he mentions is Lublin, which has already fallen to the Russians. He and his men are avoiding the bigger towns because, as he puts it, the air there contains too much lead. It is soldier speak. In general, though, he does not – and surely cannot – say much about what is going on. The implications are clear enough, however, they are fleeing and cut off. My father's last letter is from the 16th of March. In it, he admits that the situation "here" does not "look rosy" but still admonishes my mother not to be sad and hang her head.

There is no more mail or information for some time, which must have been hard on my mother as it was on so many other women. My father did make it onto a ship and ended up in an American Prisoner of War Camp. He was very lucky that his ship was not sunk by mines or bombs, as many others were, no matter if they carried fleeing women, children, or soldiers. Usually, they carried all together.

I do not remember my father ever telling us where in Germany his ship landed and where his POW camp was. When he joined us after the War, we were too young to ask and just happy to have him back with us. And later, we were too busy with our own lives. I assume he told my mother and other family members. What I do recall him saying, though, is that his POW camp only housed officers and that they were well-treated. The next note I have from my father is dated

July 24, 1945, and is short. It simply says that he has been released, is on the way home, and would first stop in Linz to see his mother and sister. He must have known that Bisamberg was occupied by the Russians and was wary, but obviously had not heard from us and did not know where we were. Once in Linz, he was then redirected to Wesenufer. His relentlessly positive outlook was really a form of magical thinking, something that carried him through.

Mother in Vienna

With my father gone during the War, my mother managed everything on her own. Moving to Vienna and furnishing an apartment as tastefully as she did when things started becoming scarce could not have been easy, but I did not notice any struggle. One day, we were there and enjoyed all the new things and comforts we had. My mother took good care of us, read to us, went on outings with us, and made sure we had other children with whom we could play. And, what was always important to her, dressed us carefully. She was strict about such things. There was no way to get around those scratchy woolen stockings in winter, complain as I might.

The Three of Us

However, I remember only one incident when she lost her temper with me. She was working in the kitchen while I did my first-grade homework. I could not grasp that, in German, the letters "e" and "u," when next to each other, were not read separately but as a diphthong. She became impatient with my lack of comprehension, snatched my doll from my hand, and threw it to the floor. The doll got nicked, and that was the end of dolls for me. My mother never slapped me, though.

Another little incident I recall reminds me of her forbearance. At Christmas in our Vienna winter, the three of us were by ourselves except for a visit to my aunt's. On the way home, my mother, probably feeling lonely, expressed disappointment that I had not given her a present. "Oh yes, I did," I quickly replied, lying and listing off a plant she had received as a gift. Of course, I soon found out who had given it to her and that she already knew all this. Yet, she said nothing. I was deeply ashamed and never forgot. Since that time, I am always quick and eager with presents.

Ironically, when my parents believed they were finally well-established and on track to the future they wanted, the end was already on the horizon and had been for some time. According to historians, Hitler and his Third Reich were doomed by 1941. But like many people around the world, my parents lacked that understanding. And, like many in Germany and Austria, they were so fully invested in the Third Reich that they did not think about what lay ahead. They felt that joining Germany through Austria's "Anschluss" offered a better future, at least initially. Then, they just held on. Their heads were buried in the sands of past experiences and their own backgrounds. They neither saw the beginning decline of the Third Reich nor did they realize what was going on behind the scenes, yet they did not look either. As I already indicated, my sense is that they were far from being fanatic national socialists, but they were also far from opposing them. This held true for both my parents, I believe. Still my mother would have had more time to inform herself, but perhaps not. She was exposed to propaganda everywhere and to all the little goodies and services the regime offered "our mothers."

For her, the decline might have become noticeable when we left the apartment with many of our possessions in it, although I do not know if it did. She took in a boarder who had been bombed out and moved us in with her parents in Bisamberg, considering it a temporary solution, not dreaming that she would spend most of the rest of her life there. As it turned out, we only stayed in the Vienna apartment during the fall and winter of 1943/44 and never returned, even if it belonged to us for much longer. I briefly went to first grade nearby, but as much as I liked the apartment, I did not regret leaving. In Vienna, there were too many air raids, although far fewer than in German cities.

My mother packed up most of our clothes as well as her china and crystal, which she stored in my grandfather's barn. After the War when Russian troops occupied Bisamberg – and parts of Vienna – soldiers found the crates, turned them over, and broke most of the content in the hope of finding…I do not know what. Later, when I was eleven or twelve, I greatly admired the few salvaged pieces which were – at the time, certainly – irreplaceable and felt sorry about the senseless destruction of the rest. Not that we needed champagne glasses just then. The experience with the wastefully broken crystal and dishes was our own little and, ultimately, insignificant story of the Russian soldiers' destructiveness when and where they took over in 1945. It was very mild in comparison to the many awful stories about the Russians' stupidity and cruelty, which were told with a mixture of horror and contemptuous glee long after the War had ended. A running gag was their love of wrist watches, three or four on each arm, which they took off of civilians.

Much more serious were the rapes, which only registered with me later. I was fascinated, though, by the story of the village priest hiding women and girls in a crypt of the graveyard. But, at least for a while, I had no idea why. Later, I also heard a rape story told as a joke at a party – by a very well-established Catholic schoolteacher, no less. This Austrian teacher claimed that an elderly spinster begged the soldiers to rape her as well, as she had never had a man. I do not know if the story was true, nor how this person knew, but it struck me as very cruel.

Negative tales about Russian behavior continued to circulate, although the soldiers soon became "orderly" occupation forces and kept to themselves. When I lived in Bisamberg after the War, I did not encounter them often but was still cautious about them. At the same time, I felt sorry for the occasional lonely soldier whom I encountered sitting by the river fishing or the few officers who came to our balls expecting to dance with us girls. We never dared refuse them, but after one dance, a friend would cut in. There was still an aura of fear and contempt surrounding them. Neither the American soldiers nor the other occupiers, the British and the French – of whom I only heard – were looked down upon the same way, nor were the women who associated with them. To be a "Russian whore" was as low as a woman could get. I knew that much, even if I had no clear understanding of what a whore was.

In Bisamberg

Apart from the short interlude in Vienna and five years between 1945 and 1950 when we were in Wesenufer and Linz, I spent not only my early childhood but also my teenage and young adult years in Bisamberg. I do not have any distinct memories of our lives in Bisamberg before our stint in the apartment though, my recollections seem to blend together in that regard. However large the Vienna apartment looms in my memory, Bisamberg and my grandparents' house defined my childhood and my youth, but never exclusively. The city was always nearby. I went there for outings, and later for school, university, to meet friends, and to attend many cultural events.

The village of Bisamberg is quite old, almost as old as Vienna. Situated along the Danube, at the foot of a small mountain by the same name, it was separated from the river by large flood plains, small woods, and fields that often flooded. Originally, the Danube had many arms along which fishing, hunting, and eventually agriculture had existed for centuries. Nomads moved through, and settlers stayed. When the Romans established their provinces of Pannonia and Noricum south of the Danube, they quickly recognized the strategic importance of "our" small mountain on the other side of the river. They built a watchtower as an outpost against invaders from the North and as preparation for further conquests on their part. Not too far down the Danube on its southern shores, they established a military camp, Vindobona, which eventually became Vienna. The major Roman settlement, Carnuntum, was even farther downriver. Schoolchildren were always taken to Carnuntum and the Roman museum there, which I found more attractive than most museums I visited as a child, because it was small and contained. Besides, it involved a major class excursion.

A first written record of an old form of the name Bisamberg appears on a document that can be dated back to the year 1108. During this period, the Danube provided an avenue for colonization and Christianization of the region from the West, from Bavaria and Franconia. Across the Danube from our hill, there is a higher mountain, the Leopoldsberg, which falls steeply towards the river and gently slopes towards Vienna. Eons ago, the Danube cut a path between that mountain and the Bisamberg and created what is called the "Wiener Pforte" [the Viennese gate]. **Thus, in terms of flora and fauna, the Bisamberg, like the Leooldsberg, belongs to the Vienna Woods, and both are extensions of the Alps. In the Middle Ages, Leopold III, Margrave of Austria, whose family, the Babenberger, had also come from the West, established the powerful monastery of Klosterneuburg at the foot of the Leopoldsberg, facing toward us, not toward Vienna. It was, and is, wealthy, owning land on our side as well. You can see the monastery dominating the landscape whenever you look at the river from the Bisamberg. It is part of a string of equally or even more impressive monasteries erected along or close to the**

Danube, such as Melk or Göttweig, which were founded to spread the Christian faith as well as new methods of cultivating the land and growing wine. The land was the source of wealth and power, and obtaining it in feudal times and thereafter depended on an ever more complex system of grants, donations, and eventually purchases. Records had to be kept, and in one such record of the donation of property in 1108, a Prun de Pusinberge is mentioned as a witness. Pusinberge goes back to "Berg des Puso" [mountain of Puso], Puso being a common Franconian name. This eventually led to Bisamberg. Thus, our village is called after the family who owned the mountain and surrounding lands.

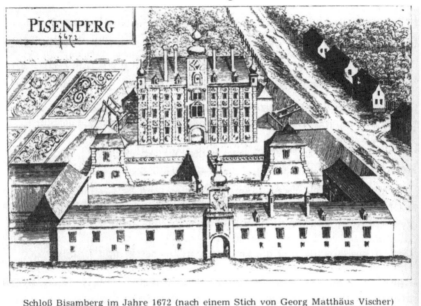

Schloß Bisamberg im Jahre 1672 (nach einem Stich von Georg Matthäus Vischer)

[Bisamberg Castle in 1627, Engraving by Vischer]

By 1203, the de Puisenberges had built a fortified manor house on the site of today's castle in the center of the village. There is also mention of a Romanesque chapel, which was fortified as well. It stood where the village church stands now, above the castle, on an outcropping of the Bisamberg. Liegemen and peasants settled around the manor house and church.

Engraving of Early Fortified Church

The village of Bisamberg is a mixture of two village types, one clustered around the church and castle, the other, a so-called "Straßendorf" [street village], stretching along a main road with barns and stables behind the houses and opening to the fields beyond.

As a student at the university I had to take a course on various types of villages and houses in the German-speaking lands. "Village" is the translation of the German word "Dorf"; the most basic form of organized settlement in the Middle Ages, with "Markt" [market] and "Stadt" [town] next in terms of rights and importance. Now, Bisamberg is a "Marktgemeinde" [market community], a designation which still has some administrative significance although no markets are being held. The "Straßendorf" is common in the flatter country to the North of Vienna and far into the East, into Hungary.

My Uncle's and his Family's Summer Home in Bisamberg

In Bisamberg, the cluster around the church makes up the oldest part, with the main street then skirting the mountain and following the model of the "Straßendorf," but with the mountain in the back of one side. In my childhood, many of the houses on the mountain side were no longer farms but small villas. The biggest belonged to the family into which my aunt married. As a small child and even later on, I often visited it and was always intrigued by its layout, a combination of turn-of-the-19th-century beauty and practicality. There was a very formal front garden with high-stem rose bushes in a rondeau surrounded by a circular gravel drive, well fenced-in, of course, with dark double lilacs running along the fence. Behind the house, a large flower and vegetable garden and a tennis court stretched to another fence, which marked the steep ascent to the mountain and was intended to keep out deer and hares. From there, a serpentine path led to the woods on top of the mountain, where there was yet another fence. Fruit trees and berry bushes stretched uphill towards it. I loved the place, even if it lost some of its elegance towards the end of the war, with the tennis court being turned into a potato field.

Over the centuries, the fortress and the church were expanded and rebuilt several times until they became the small Renaissance castle and the baroque church they were in my childhood and still are today. Ownership of the castle, its land holdings, and the large vineyard frequently changed hands until it came to the Abensberg-Traun family, one of the oldest once-noble families in Austria. They also possessed – and still do – much more spectacular castles and fortresses in Upper and Lower Austria, and during my childhood, they took no interest in the one in Bisamberg. In 1961, they sold it to a furniture manufacturer; the small park was used to build fancy condominiums. Even if older people still referred to the owners as "die Herrschaft" [the masters], the family never stayed or visited. Still, until 1961 there must have been a manager because when I was a child, the fields, woods, and the large vineyard with its prominently situated cellar were being worked. Eventually, it was sold, not only the castle and park but everything else as well. Much of the land was subdivided into housing parcels gently sloping up the northern side of the mountain and turning the village of Bisamberg into the desirable Viennese suburb it is now—if you own a car. I had left by then, but on one of my visits, my mother asked me to drive her around that area so she could see all the changes to what she had previously known as only fields and woods.

Theoretically, the whole area is part of a green zone around Vienna and may not be built up, a regulation established as far back as 1905 to guarantee the Viennese population access to green spaces. The regulation is still in effect and does not allow smaller landowners to develop property on the mountain. My grandfather's vineyard, for example, had to be let go into shrubland when it could no longer be worked on.

Nonetheless, the Abensberg-Trauns somehow still had enough influence to circumvent these restrictions. However, I do not know the details; I was never interested in the castle and its owners, which is strange because, as a child and later on in life, I liked to speculate about interesting buildings, how they looked inside, and the people who lived or had lived there. Yet, the Bisamberg castle held no fascination, perhaps because when I was a child, it appeared lifeless and because, without reflecting on it, the idea of a "Herrschaft" was distasteful to me. Only recently, when I looked up the history of the village, did I also learn about that of the castle. While I was growing up, nobody cared about it, certainly nobody in my family nor anyone in school. However earlier, the "Turnverein" [gymnastics club] of the village, which was a center of social activity for my parents when they were young, apparently did and could use the enclosed front yard of the castle for some of their events.

The village church is a different story. I loved it and the surrounding sites as a little girl, even if I did not know about their history either. My grandparents, my parents, and now my younger brother are buried in the graveyard over which the church watches, i.e., they have a marked grave. Many others from my grandparents' families lie there as well, but very old graves have been let go because of limited space. When I recently attended my younger brother's funeral, I was reminded how strong my ties still are to the place, how beautiful it is, and how strangely at home I feel there. The church is Catholic, of course, and a little baroque gem of which there are many in the region, but none is as beautifully situated.

Briefly, at the height of the Reformation, it had "changed hands" and turned Lutheran but quickly reverted. The church can only be reached via steep uphill paths and steps leading to its entrance. In the 1600s, a lady of the manor who resided in the castle had one access path built into a staircase with life-size statues representing the stations of the cross, a "Kreuzweg." A few steps down is/was the "Schlosskeller" (the castle cellar), where, at the time of my youth, you could sit and drink wine. As is the custom, certainly in Austria, the church, the graveyard, and a place to drink, eat and make merry are never far apart. A little lower than the church and nestled into the mountain were, and still are, small, very old farmhouses. Some have their wine cellars right below the living quarters. If you walk further up the mountain, you come to the "Waldandacht" [wood devotional], a path through the woods along which saints' images and small altars are attached to the trees. The whole area was and, to a certain degree, still is steeped in traditional rural Catholicism, which approached God through nature and images.

Baroque Stations of the Cross

Although, towards the end of the War, my mother felt more secure in Bisamberg with her parents, I wonder if the village was indeed safer than downtown Vienna. The mountain, or really, hill, the Bisamberg, which had given the village its name, is a low-flung promontory, rising no more than 400 yards. Despite its lack of elevation, it has continued to hold strategic importance for centuries. During this war, it housed FLAK [air defense] installations; earlier, there had been trenches – still traceable – against the Swedes (in the Thirty Years War) and the French (during the Napoleonic Wars), all intended to defend the city of Vienna farther down the Danube. In my time, there were other desirable targets nearby as well, such as an oil refinery and a shipyard.

While our village bore the name of the mountain and lay at the foot of its highest elevation, other small villages, some nearer to Vienna, surrounded the gentler extensions to the north and east and were probably somewhat safer. Planes came from the West and approached Vienna on our side of the Danube because the Vienna Woods, on the other side, had higher peaks and stretched all the way to the Alps. By 1944, air raids had increased in frequency, even if we continued to suffer less than many areas in Germany. Still, I will never forget the penetrating sound of the air raid sirens or the all-clear indicating that planes were turning back, occasionally with one or two bombs left to drop. The FLAK must have been somewhat effective, for at one point, our village was permitted, even encouraged, to go see the wreckage of a plane that had been shot down and lay in a nearby field. I was stunned by how fragile it appeared. There was no trace of the pilot, and I wondered what had happened to him. Had he been killed, or had he bailed and been captured? There were no traces of blood or of a parachute. "Silk" from parachutes became readily available at the time. My mother dyed it and used it for blouses and skirts.

The two-class Primary School I attended in Bisamberg continued to have school into early 1945, but many children had to repeat a grade when instruction started up again in the fall. My mother saw to it that I did not, although I missed even more than my classmates as I was assigned the task of sitting in the teacher's office and listening to the radio for early warnings of approaching planes. This way, we had more time to get to a shelter. Even if my assignment was a bit boring, it was less so than class. Besides, I was proud of it and felt important.

I do not recall which of the available shelters we went to, the one in the school or the one right across the street which was for everybody. Bisamberg used its wine cellars as air-raid shelters, and this one was built into the mountain right in the center of the village. It was very large and had been set up with benches, first aid kits, and a warden who was in charge. I much preferred it to the dark basement in Vienna to which we had to climb down many narrow stairs and where we sat with strangers. Now everything was familiar. Sometimes when we were not in school, my mother even took us to our own wine cellar. It was quite large as well but more remote and secluded. My grandparents never came with us anywhere, despite my grandmother's general anxiousness. They stayed home or in their vineyard, which was just as good because none of the cellars we frequented could have withstood a serious hit, but neither could the designated shelter we went to in the city. The basement there may have been deep enough, but if a whole apartment house collapsed onto it, people would be trapped. I suffered from claustrophobia even as a child. Was there a tunnel connecting to another house, as was the case in some of those basement shelters? I did not know. At any rate, I did feel better in Bisamberg, where the alarms seemed to me to be more of an exciting distraction.

The planes which flew in over our little village aimed for more important targets. Still, with all that was nearby, there was always the possibility of collateral damage. One time, a classmate and I came out of the shelter and found her house, a rare apartment building in the village, reduced to rubble with dust still swirling around. It was the first bombed-out house I ever saw. Later, when we lived in Linz, I would come across many ruins, and still later, when I visited London, I would happen on a part of town that was completely destroyed, something I had never seen in Austria. This first pile of jagged walls and debris remained most vividly with me, though, because I still wonder at my child's reaction. Rather than pity my friend, who had lost her home and was crying for her doll, which she had left behind, I felt envy that something so distinctive was happening to her. I still had little understanding of the situation and must have considered myself and my family invulnerable. In part, that may have been due to my mother, who kept us on an even keel and heeded my father's constant admonitions in his letters to stay calm and cheerful. She did so even as the front came ever closer. Thus, our lives appeared normal and all too ordinary to me, but change would soon come to us as well.

My grandfather's house was on a little then unpaved street which abutted onto Highway One, the main thoroughfare from East to West along our side of the Danube. There was a small grocery store on the corner where I was often sent to get milk or rolls. On one of my errands in the early spring of 1945, I saw something extraordinary: a seemingly endless stream of covered wagons moving by. Since then, I have only seen such wagons in US films about settlers going West. In my memory, the caravan was eerily quiet, although it could not have been. There were no cars, though. I was fascinated as I stood there watching for a while and then running home to tell my mother. I must have been given some explanation, but I do not recall it. Did I understand that what I saw was the harbinger of an end? I was not afraid, but no matter what I was told, I sensed that flight was in the air and that this orderly-seeming trek was a sign of major changes to come.

As an adult, I studied the literature and history of this period and read much about the chaotic flight of ethnic Germans from areas in the East, where they had lived for centuries in relatively peaceful, if uneasy, cohabitation with older local populations. Hitler was not the first to seek "Lebensraum" [space to live] for Germans in the East. Colonizing, originally hand in hand with Christianizing, went back far. However, Hitler's methods of invasion and occupation, from which most ethnic Germans and the carpetbaggers who moved in with the occupying German troops had profited, built so much resentment that they were all driven out as soon as the Soviet army advanced. It did not matter how many generations had lived and usually prospered in the respective areas. Later, I also learned that the refugees in my childhood memories who came along the Danube – and mostly stopped somewhere in Austria – were much better off than the ones further north, where the treks were more chaotic and, indeed, more horrific than what I saw. Still, the image of the wagons inexorably moving down the road in search of new places to settle is seared into my memory. It gave me an early, if vague, sense of the insecurity of home and the never-ending need for flight or migration. Very soon, we would also flee.

My Bisamberg Grandparents: Grandfather

My mother's parents stayed, of course. Bisamberg was the world to which they belonged; my grandmother, perhaps, in a more emotionally profound manner than my grandfather. They had vineyards and fruit gardens and made their living that way. For them, leaving was not an option, although many of the people in the covered wagons had lived off their land as well. However, ultimately, my grandparents were even more deeply rooted than they had been. Their forbears had not moved for centuries, except in my grandmother's family, from one neighboring village to the next. Long before I was born, she had owned a general store and the milk collection for the village, but my grandfather had never wanted anything to do with catering to customers. He was a handsome, proud, and taciturn man who served his obligatory military service with the Hoch- und Deutschmeister, Vienna's house regiment. He was even invited to stay on, which would have made for an easier life, but he wanted to be as independent as he possibly could be— nobody should have been able to tell him what to do.

According to my mother, he even thought of emigrating to America, probably after WWI, but considered himself too old and remained to live through another war. He had already been too old to serve in World War I. His family went back for many generations in Bisamberg. Their name, Zauninger, shows up in the village's earliest written records from the 1700s.

By then, the family must have been well-established as winemakers, fruit growers, and as innkeepers because they sometimes served as mayors and village judges. When the lords of the manor gave up the hunt, which had been theirs since feudal times, men from the village, including a Zauninger, founded a hunting society and took over. Owning a hunt was no small thing; just having some land did not automatically give you the right to shoot game on it. My grandfather was still a member of this hunting society and brought home an occasional hare. There were no more deer left when I grew up. I have a picture of him posing with his proud partners and remember his beautiful hunting dog, if only vaguely, but with the respect of a small child. My grandfather did not replace him and stopped hunting when I was still a little girl. Over the centuries, the Zauninger family also regularly provided a priest or nun to the Catholic Church. But when my grandfather died at the age of 91, he was the last male with that name. His younger brother had passed away long before him.

The Bisamberg Hunt with Grandfather Standing Second from Right

My grandfather was a "good" Catholic, but even so, he was more enlightened than many in the countryside. He sent his two daughters to school way beyond what was mandatory then and made sure that they received a professional education with which they could support themselves. This was not free and not at all customary among his fellow vintners and farmers, but it served my mother and aunt very well. They both got married – the usual argument was that anything more than rudimentary education for women was a waste as they would not use it. But they kept relying on their schooling. My aunt, who attended a commercial college, helped run her and her husband's business, and my mother, who graduated from a series of institutes specializing in fashion design and dress, coat, and even hat-making, freelanced as a young woman. Although she never worked for pay after her marriage, her friends and family (including her daughter) counted on her valuable skills, which were especially sought after during the war and its aftermath. When I was growing up, she tried to teach me a few things about sewing, but my interest and talent were quite limited; she could do things so much better. I could show her a dress I liked in a shop window or magazine, and she would come up with a pattern with changes she or I suggested to make it fit perfectly. Then, ready-made clothes were not that common and not available in so many different sizes as today.

In spring, summer, and fall, my grandfather worked hard outdoors, but what he did was varied and demanded thought and planning, which he invested in ample measure. His properties were some distance apart, and walking back and forth kept him slim and limber. In his late eighties, he still hiked up to his major vineyard on the Bisamberg on a path so steep that, nowadays, nobody uses it anymore. As a child and into my teens, I loved that vineyard very much. My grandfather had another one close to the village, which was smaller, but still vast to us children and enticing in different ways. The land was steeper there, so he had terraced it himself and had dedicated different levels to different crops. Besides the vines, which did not produce grapes as good as those in the vineyard further up, there were many fruit trees, berry bushes such as currants and gooseberries, and peonies everywhere. His were the dark red so-called "peasant" peonies, which I still love but rarely find. My grandfather cut them when the flower heads were firmly closed and put them in his basement until dealers came to pick them up and ferry them to markets in Vienna. Later in the spring and summer, these same or other dealers came to get the fruit, cherries, apricots, peaches, pears, gooseberries, and currants. For some reason, we had only apples for our own use. My grandmother arranged the fruit in wooden crates making sure that, when possible, the best-looking pieces, which she even polished, were right on top.

On all his properties, my grandfather used his land most efficiently and economically. Not only were his gardens and even the vineyards multipurposed, but he also planted large trees, like walnut trees, at the edge of his land so that their shade would not use up too much of his space. This was a controversial aspect of his practices but, I assume, was quite common. Any neighbor had the right to gather the fruit that hung into their field or garden and cut the branches that bothered them. I remember the enormous walnut tree which stood in the corner of the entry to our house and covered the road as well as our neighbor's garden. When it was time to harvest the nuts, long poles were used to beat them down. There was very little space in our entryway where they could fall, so most landed on the roadway in front of our house and in our neighbor's garden. He always came to watch that we did not enter it and collect "his" nuts. None of the adults did, but my brother and I climbed in when he was not watching. These walnuts were large and precious because nuts are essential to many Viennese cakes and cookies, and my mother used them regularly. We never sold any but kept them in burlap sacks and hung them up so neither mice nor mold would get to them.

In contrast to the walnut trees, which threw large and dense shadows, the tiny peach trees which dotted the big vineyard caused no shade to speak of. They bore small furry green balls, which were not good to eat raw but delicious when peeled and canned. I have never seen them anywhere since then. Even in the large vineyard, my grandfather followed his principle of multipurposed use and set aside a section for varied fruit trees and berry bushes. A large cherry tree dominated that area, which my grandfather had grafted, so it bore three different kinds of cherries, May cherries were the first, then you went higher and higher to get later and sweeter varieties. Unfortunately, since my grandfather did not spray his trees, the fruit often developed worms.

Soaking the cherries in water got the worms to swim on top so they could be poured off. This disgusted me, but at least I knew that, when my mother cooked something with cherries (cherry strudel was my favorite), there were no more worms to worry about. Eating the cherries raw was a bit more problematic for finicky me. I always opened them up to check and got my hands and clothes smeared with red juice. To pick fruit, my grandfather used large, heavy wooden ladders, which he stored in his gardens and his house. They took considerable strength and skill to move and handle. My brother later learned to do that, but as children, we just clambered up the trees, although picking cherries was not our favorite occupation because it took so long to fill a basket.

The large vineyard was called "Grübel" (Grube meaning 'pit' or 'depression') because it was in an indentation on the steepest part of the Bisamberg and, thus, particularly well-suited for growing things. It caught the sun and kept the dirt from washing away. In its center, my grandfather had built a wooden hut with a bench inside and another one along its front with an arbor of vines providing shade. It took me a while to get used to the hut where tools were stored, and burlap sacks and bunches of onion and garlic were hung. The hut smelled of all these things but also of dust and mice. Not far from it, my grandfather had dug a little cellar to keep his wine, his food, and some water for us children. He always filled a bottle with water for us and himself at a spring at the bottom of the steep path up and called it mountain wine. We thought it was better than any other water. Watching him eat his late-morning snack, mostly bread and a hunk of bacon or ham, was fascinating for us children. It's hard to describe: he held everything in one hand, cut little pieces with his pocketknife in his other hand, and then ate them with this hand, which still held the pocketknife. He did not need a plate or cutting board. Fruit would be available from late May on.

Klosterneuburg with Danube in Background

As a child and teenager, the "Grübel" was one of my two favorite places. It had a spectacular view of the Danube. Upriver, there would be two castles, Greifenstein and Kreuzenstein, facing each other. One was a ruin; the other had been rebuilt during the late 19th-century craze for everything medieval. Supposedly, pieces from all over Europe had been collected for its reconstruction. Less probable is the story that, during the fifteenth and sixteenth centuries, when knights resorted to waylaying travelers, a chain spanned the Danube from one castle to the other, to hold up the many ships going up or down the river. It would have had to be a very long chain, but some less elaborate form of robbery is quite probable. In my childhood, Kreuzenstein, which we sometimes visited, was set up as a museum – it still is today. It always struck me as dusty and lifeless, yet in my imagination, I filled it with visions of how ladies and their knights lived in an idealized medieval world. When we were old enough to go there by ourselves on our bikes, my brother and I preferred to climb around in the deep moat, which no longer held water. We rarely went to Greifenstein because you had to cross the Danube, which took much more time and cost money for the ferry.

From the vineyard, you also saw the imposing abbey of Klosterneuburg right across the Danube at the foot of Vienna's "house mountain," the Leopoldsberg. Its gentle side, which we could not see, sloped towards Vienna and was also covered with vineyards. I say "also," but as far as Vienna is concerned, these vineyards are the ones that matter and the ones through which Viennese take their Sunday excursions and to which tourists are taken to taste the wine. On our side, the part facing the Leopoldsberg's steep descent went down sharply as well, but fields and inundation areas then stretched quite a ways before you got to the river. We needed bikes to go swimming and bathing by the Danube. On the Klosterneuburg side, there is only a small rim of wetlands, and the street and railroad are close to the Danube, as are summer cottages. It was/is easily accessible from Vienna and, in the early twentieth century, became a popular place for Viennese to go on summer days and weekends if they wanted water and not just the woods of the *Wiener Wald*.

The family still owns my grandfather's vineyard, but it quickly grew into scrubby woods when it was no longer tended to. Later, I lived far away, but I dreamt of having it cleared and turned into a garden that I could visit and from which I could look out, just as I had done as a child and teenager. It was a fantasy, but it pleased me to hear that my nephew, who lived close by, entertained the same pipe dream. Some years ago, my older brother and I literally slid down from the top of the Bisamberg's *Elisabethhöhe* – named after the famous empress Sisy who had visited it once – and searched for a way into this former vineyard. We managed by crawling through brambles and in between gnarled trees but found no place from which we had a view nor anything we recognized from earlier times, only traces of animals that had found shelter in the underbrush. Unless somebody can build a house and live there, which is not allowed, the property will remain our and our children's contribution to a little wilderness in the green zone around Vienna, which is a good thing. Seeing the mountainside dotted with houses and having fences impede wildlife is not the legacy I would want for my grandfather.

"Weinlese"

My Grandfahter Supervising Grape Harvest

In a vineyard, the big event of the year was, and is, "Weinlese" [grape harvest, récolte], which takes place around the beginning of October. A small vintner like my grandfather would call on extended family and friends, including city folks, for help. All they were "paid" with was a bucket of grapes and two good meals, but they came gladly. Our male cousin remembered the event so fondly that much later, when he was a Lutheran minister and social worker in Germany, he signed on with a vintner in our area to help with the harvest. It was a form of vacation for him.

My brother and I were about eleven and twelve when we started participating "seriously," as did our cousin. I was with the women, who cut the grapes off the vines and filled individual buckets, which we then poured into larger wooden "Butten" [grape hods]. The boys and men carried these on their backs up to a spot above the vineyard where a cart with two very large barrels was parked. They poured the grapes in and returned.

Cousin Horst and Putzi (Richard) during "Weinlese"

Towards the end of the day, the farmer who had been hired to provide the cart, brought two horses back up from the village to pull the cart down the mountain to our wine cellar. They used a path that led to the village center and was less steep than the way we usually went up but still quite perilous. Even so, for us children, it was fun to ride down on the rim of the vats. At our cellar, the grapes had to be shoveled back into the hods and carried down to the wine press. As I remember it all, I am struck by how labor-intensive this age-old process was. It has changed considerably since then, as have the implements used, my grandfather probably being one of the last traditional vintners to employ the old tools. Yet, wine-making still relies on tradition, hard work, and careful planning, as well as coordination. And it may have retained some of the festive harvest atmosphere – at least among smaller vintners – that it had for us as youngsters and for the adults as well. My memories are, of course, tinged with nostalgia, but the excitement and enjoyment are unforgettable. Mine was not the hard work, though.

The Cellar and "Heuriger"

My grandfather's wine cellar, which he shared with two others who may have only stored their wines (I never saw any activity), was enormous, or so it appeared to me. Long ago, it had supposedly belonged to a large Viennese wine merchant. You entered and descended a few steps through a little building set into the mountainside, the "press house." Ours had one small window and a big double door for which we had gigantic keys. There was electric light, which was probably something my grandfather had introduced, and a concrete floor, but no wine press – the one we had was far too big for this small space.

Instead, you could sit down at a picnic table in case it rained. In addition, tables, benches, wine glasses, and special wine bottles were stored there for times when my grandfather hosted a "Heuriger," a special, long-standing custom in Vienna and its surrounding wine-growing regions. Vintners were/are each allotted a period of the year during which they are allowed to sell their new wine directly to people coming through and stopping for a glass or more – and some food. The fact that the place is open for customers is announced on special boards in the villages and by hanging a small bundle of pine brush over the door to the cellar or house where the wine is to be sold. "Ausgsteckt" is the Austrian term for it, which is hard to translate appropriately, but means something like "pinned up for display." During my grandfather's time, many people still brought their own snacks, but he always had cheese, ham, and delicious home-baked bread for those who did not. From the age of twelve on, I served as his waitress. It was a weekend afternoon and early evening undertaking and fun too.

Heuriger in 1929 with Grandfather and Grandmother in the Door of a Presshouse which was later Rebuilt

Recent Heuriger in Bisamberg at Night

The custom of "Heuriger" [new wine – from grapes pressed during the previous fall] has not lost its age-old popularity. On the contrary, rich and poor, young and old, still enjoy it. "Heurige" on the outskirts as well as within the city limits of Vienna can be reached by public transportation, perhaps with a little walk. When the weather is nice, people sit outdoors at long tables, eat, drink, and talk. Sometimes, at fancier establishments, there is music, a zither or a fiddle, but all the people I knew and know prefer them "quiet." On our side of the Danube, the "Heurigen" are less fashionable, if you can use that word, than on the other, but a bit cheaper. Tourists and tourist buses do not make it there, but the Viennese who "know" do. A "real Heuriger" cannot operate year-round, in contrast to a country inn, but, of course, it needs an indoor space for cooler weather. In the past, the vintners who used their own yards and houses emptied some rooms for the duration, including their bedroom, which was often the biggest room in the house. Then, the guests sat and drank under the saint, Virgin Mary, or other religious painting that had been left hanging in its place over the vintner couple's beds when these were temporarily removed. This always intrigued me but did not seem to bother anybody else.

Nowadays, the set-ups are more elaborate than in my youth, and some establishments, even on "our side," are architect-designed. There is one place in Bisamberg, though, which has newly built spaces indoors and out, but also uses the bedroom and kitchen of the original tiny farmhouse. The owners have long since moved to more spacious quarters but know full well that many people enjoy a touch of quaintness. These days, a variety of wines is being served everywhere, not just all-new vintages. There is also a large selection of very good home-cooked country food available, buffet-style. People no longer bring their own snacks. Indeed, a meal at a "Heuriger" is often better and usually cheaper than one in an inn. At my grandfather's "Heuriger," everything was still very simple; there were a few tables with benches outside his cellar along a small road up the mountain. Beyond, the path narrowed, and the woods started. He served only one kind of wine made of a combination of grapes. "Gemischter Satz" [mixed vintage] is the fashionable word now that a combination of varietals has become popular again. For my grandfather and his generation, planting different kinds of grapes was a precaution. Some kinds might do better than others in certain years. Nowadays, the "Gemischter Satz" is sold along varietals such as "Grüner Veltliner," which is THE grape associated with our area and my favorite. Many of the younger vintners – there are now women as well as men – have studied viniculture at Klosterneuburg, which has turned its centuries-old tradition of winemaking and fruit growing into a renowned school. My grandfather's books on grafting and wine-making already came from there.

Our press house also stored candles, iron candle holders, and, unfortunately, forever damp matches, all of which you needed as you went down into the cellar proper, where there was only a light bulb at the entrance, then deep darkness. It was wonderfully exciting for me as a child to walk into it, but not scary, perhaps because I was never alone. In the cellar, the floor was dirt, and the ceiling was vaulted brick. I do not know when it was built, but it was quite old and had that wonderful smell of wine, mold, and cool dampness, which, to me, does have an odor as well.

To get from the press house into the cellar, you had to go down a bit deeper through a small, steep vaulted incline of which I am reminded when I see Friedrich Murnau's *Nosferatu*; only there does the hero walk up through such a vault. The door fitted into this passageway was also like the one in the film. Stepping through it, the cellar proper stretched before you, high and seemingly vast. I have only been in similar, albeit much larger and deeper cellars in Klosterneuburg, which go back to the 1200s. As you entered, you could see our gigantic wooden wine press standing on the left. Many years later, I came across one like it in a museum in Burgundy. After the press, long rows of wooden barrels stretched into the darkness. Each owner arranged them according to size. It was – and still is, when you can see it – a very pleasing sight, suggesting harvest, order, and prosperity, and somehow did so to me even as a child. My grandfather's row was the last, with a kind of well at the very end. When we were little, we were always warned about it because you only saw it when you came close and had a candle in your hand. All it was, though – we soon realized – was a brick-encased opening, which turned out to be quite shallow and held no water. Perhaps at one point, it really had been a well.

Next to his smallest barrel, my grandfather had set up a table with chairs where he could sit down, taste the wine, and have a snack – after he had wiped off the white film which covered the wood. As squeamish as I was, this never bothered me. To retrieve wine and manipulate it, my grandfather used a "Weinheber" [wine siphon] made of glass. It had a thin, very long pipe on one end and a bulbous part at the other. With it, he could reach from the top deep into a barrel, siphon up some wine, and squirt it into a glass for tasting or into another barrel to top that off. He handled his "Weinheber" very skillfully and carefully. It was handblown and must have been costly. Still, he had three of these siphons, one in the cellar, one in the press house, and one at his home, where there was a small wine cellar off the regular basement under the house. Being sent down there to retrieve a bottle or fill a pitcher for dinner was scarier for me than going into the darkness of the big cellar.

My grandfather eventually taught us how to use a siphon, although he never let us drink wine. He also taught us that a barrel had to always be kept full for the wine to remain good. Thus, he had to move it around. To bring wine home, he used a very large glass bottle encased in a basket weave so it would not break easily. It held ten or more liters and was carefully transported on a little cart. The walk from the cellar to the house took more than half an hour. We all used our bikes to go back and forth, but my grandfather did not. He walked everywhere and pulled the cart when there was something large to transport. He had no horses, having little use for them. Occasionally, when he needed horses, he rented them or bartered for them. By the way, unlike many of the farmers and vintners who visited their wine cellars to drink and sometimes ended up in a ditch – at least, I heard stories about great uncles and other relatives who did – my grandfather only went to his cellar to work and check on things. As far as I know, he never had too much to drink.

When we were teenagers, we were finally allowed to have the "Haustrunk" [housedrink], which he and the family had every day with meals. It was made of a second pressing of the grapes and contained little alcohol but was much more refreshing than stale water. It was on the sour, or more elegantly, dry side, as was our wine. Unlike many vintners, my grandfather did not add sugar to his wine, even when, in certain years, it was quite "dry." Supposedly, you could tell that you had wine with added sugar by the headache you got the next morning.

 Long after my grandfather and even my father, who tried to carry on for a few years by hiring somebody to help with the vineyard, there was a big scandal involving large Austrian wine producers who were not satisfied with sugar but used refrigerator coolant to make their wines taste sweet and smooth. This scandal led to a total overhaul of Austria's wine production and, eventually, made the wines much better. Sweet they are not, but most people in Austria do not care for sweet wines.

Although my grandfather's methods for wine and fruit growing were what you would call *green*, he did spray his vines. The fruit trees only received a sticky sleeve around their trunks to protect them – somewhat. I was very interested in his work, but despite his general open-mindedness towards girls and his pride in my school learning, he did not pass his vinicultural and horticultural skills on to me, nor to my mother and aunt before me. My older brother, however, received as much instruction as he would absorb, even if my grandfather did not expect him to follow in his footsteps. I think he knew full well that his own way of being independent and making a living was doomed and was very much in favor of our going to university. In his dealings with us, he was always patient and never shouted. Perhaps we all learned from him and his quiet ways. When he was unhappy with something one of us did, including my mother and grandmother, he would clam up and not talk for a while. This did not worry us as kids but was probably hard to bear for the adults. My grandmother made no secret of the fact that she would have liked to have her husband be a bit chattier.

In the late fall, my grandfather went around the village to help people make Sauerkraut. It appears he was the only one who had a large plane with which to slice cabbage heads. I watched him when he made Sauerkraut for us. He had a special wooden vat into which he put layer after layer of sliced cabbage, perhaps adding – but I am not sure – sliced onions and certainly salt with a bit of cumin. He then closed the vat tightly with specially fitted wooden pieces, which exerted pressure on the contents. I do not know how long the cabbage had to ferment, but when it was ready, we had tasty Sauerkraut, which would last us all winter.

Among my grandfather's many old tools – I wonder what happened to them; probably they just rotted away over time – he also owned a special mill to finely grind poppy seeds. He grew poppies all over his vineyard and hung the pods up to dry. Poppy seeds, particularly when they are very finely ground, are an important ingredient in several traditional Austrian dishes. My grandfather's mill was in high demand in the village. Even the grocer – of course, a cousin of my mother's – often sent for it.

Like many other families, we stored food over the winter, such as our own potatoes for which a section in the basement was reserved – right next to the coal for the stoves. By the time spring came around, my grandfather would dig up new potatoes. They had to be scraped before boiling, not peeled, and were served with butter and parsley. It was a true delicacy when last year's potatoes were no longer appealing. My mother also reserved a corner in the basement where she piled up coarse sand to store carrots and other root vegetables like celery roots and parsnips. Apples – we did not sell them but had enough for us – were laid out on large wooden boards suspended from the cellar ceiling. Onions, garlic, corn, and even grapes and hams were hung from poles that spanned a large verandah my grandfather had built for himself to sleep in the summer and to store food in the winter.

Whenever my grandfather did not tinker or build things during the winter months, he read. He did not have what you would call a library, except for his few books on vini- and horticulture. For the rest, people gave or lent him books. There was also the custom of the daily newspapers serializing recent works of fiction. He subscribed to the conservative "Volksblatt" [People's Paper] and followed whatever novel it printed. In addition, acquaintances cut out and carefully bound together the novels which appeared in other newspapers and passed that around. When we moved into my grandparents' house after the War, I also found gold-embossed volumes of 19th-century novellas. Even then, I thought them to be awful, yet I devoured them anyway and kept puzzling about one story in which a young woman got pregnant by sitting on the balcony. However, I also came across editions of the "classics," Goethe, Schiller, and other writers who fell into that category. I know my grandfather read them because he occasionally quoted from them. However, I am not sure about the novellas. Perhaps only my grandmother was interested in sentimental 19th-century stories, some of which may have been left behind by their summer guests. My grandparents did not have the bourgeois habit of bookcases. Whatever was left eventually ended up in the attic, a wonderful place for me in which to rummage around as a young teenager.

During the years I knew my grandfather, I never asked myself if he was happy or content with his life, but then, children rarely asked themselves these questions about their elders. To me, he appeared to rest completely in himself and his way of being. Only in his very old age, when he was briefly bedridden and impatient to die, did he become visibly dissatisfied and difficult. He kept calling for my mother just when we sat down to dinner, which made my father angry.

When my grandfather called, it was always my older brother who quickly got up since he could lift and handle him. My mother never forgot that. It made him her favorite, if he did not already hold that place. However, neither I nor my younger brother suffered. It was just something I sensed and accepted. I do not know if my younger brother felt the same. He certainly became the one who spent the most time with my mother in her old age and cared for her and the house. He stayed close to home, while my older brother and I did not.

To return to my grandfather, in his last months, he was clearly tired of living and tried to force his death by sending me for the village priest to come and give him last unction. I remember running excitedly into the village center to summon the priest. My grandfather then gathered us around his bed and said goodbye. Only, he did not die. This happened a few times until he finally succeeded in passing on. I respected, even admired my grandfather, and still do; he struck me as an unusual man, rooted in his place and time, rural Austria of the late 19th century, yet forward-looking and independent-minded.

Grandmother

My grandmother was quite different. When I was a little girl, I was very close to her and loved her very much. I never heard my grandparents fight, nor did I notice them talking with each other much. They reached their golden wedding anniversary, a big event then because few people lived long enough. On that day, there was a celebration in the village church, and various government entities sent gifts, congratulatory telegrams, and even some larger coins stuck into a card. My grandmother enjoyed all of that very much. Small, without teeth, and with her usual kerchief around her hair as well as an apron around her waist is how I remember her, but she had once been a rural businesswoman in her own right. She came from a large, well-established family, which was spread out over our village and adjoining ones. Most of them were well-to-do farmers with vineyards and wine cellars on the side. My mother had so many uncles, aunts, and cousins in Bisamberg and surrounding villages that I could never keep track of them, especially since large family gatherings were not customary.

When my mother talked to her older relatives, she always addressed them formally, as was the norm. We did see them around the village, but there was little interaction, perhaps because there were too many of them, perhaps by getting a professional education and marrying my father, who clearly did not belong – nor did he want to – my mother had moved "apart."

Yet, she was always polite, and occasionally, when we were small, she took us to a relative's house, which I enjoyed very much. However, such visits stopped altogether after the War. Still, at my mother's funeral, her Bisamberg cousins attended and stayed for the customary post-funeral get-together. I did recognize them and realized that they were well-informed about my brothers and me, and indeed, you could always be sure that the extended family and the whole village knew more about you than you about them.

There were two cousins, though, with whom my mother stayed in closer contact, one on my grandmother's side, and one on my grandfather's, perhaps because they were both poor in different ways. Resi, as we called the first, never aunt Resi, had a slightly underdeveloped son, no husband, and worked odd jobs. My mother hired her as a washerwoman and for other tasks, but she always worked alongside her. Come to think of it, I do not really know how she was related and if perhaps she – as well as her son – were illegitimate. My mother treated her kindly and sometimes gave her clothes and even food, but with my child senses, I felt that Resi bore a kind of stigma in the village, perhaps "only" that of poverty and single motherhood.

The cousin on my grandfather's side, Aunt Rosi, was at the other end of the village's social spectrum. She was the only daughter of my grandfather's long-deceased brother and lived in a beautiful house that her parents had furnished for her. When I visited as a child, she, her mother, and her son only used the kitchen and some other rooms downstairs. The upstairs, of which I saw no more than glimpses, was a kind of movie set which was kept immaculately clean and orderly, but not used.

Aunt Rosi's husband had been a businessman distributing films to the country cinemas in the area, but he did not thrive and died relatively young. My grandmother called him a carpetbagger, i.e., the German/Austrian equivalent: "Zuagraster." Although the family fortunes dwindled rapidly and they were deeply in debt, Aunt Rosi and her mother kept up appearances and held on to the house, even if they sometimes went hungry, as Rosi confided to my mother, who told me and helped her cousin a bit. The son was around my brother's age, but we never played with him. I do not know why. Perhaps my mother thought that the family put on airs and pretended to be well-off and elegant. She hated pretensions of any sort and did not want us to fall under that kind of influence. Much older family jealousies between my grandmother and her sister-in-law, Rosi's mother, may also have lingered. My grandmother may have resented the fuss with which this sister-in-law surrounded her only daughter. She probably considered herself and her two daughters more substantive in their aspirations and less taken in by show. However, as a child, I only felt a certain tension when we visited and was glad to leave. At the same time, I was impressed by the household's apparent elegance.

Grandmother in Old Age and on a Pilgrimage with Resi on her Right,
Mother on her Left, and a Cousin Behind her

My grandmother was a traditional country woman. While my grandfather went into the city occasionally, she did not. In her younger years, she enjoyed going on pilgrimages to shrines and churches in the surrounding countryside. I have a picture of her with my mother and Resi, who, as girls, had apparently been invited to come along. They are all dressed up and pose in front of the church they have just visited, probably a backdrop in the photographer's studio. In the picture, my grandmother stands out as a handsome and proud-looking woman. She was a truly pious Catholic, but a pilgrimage was also entertainment for her. Not only did she have herself photographed, but she also bought mementos, such as images of saints and their horrific sufferings, which she then put between the pages of her well-worn prayer book. When I was still quite small, I loved leafing through it and looking at these gruesome but fascinating pictures. My grandmother also had a beautiful rosary with which she let me play while she taught me that different beads called for different prayers.

In the month of May, which is dedicated to Mary, the mother of Christ, I was allowed to join my grandmother for the "Maiandachten" [May devotions]. These afternoon services, which she regularly attended, continued throughout the Third Reich. Indeed, not much, if anything, in the Third Reich touched my grandmother and her daily routines or customs. Yet, eventually, it would deal her the harshest blow possible by claiming both her beloved older grandsons. The May services were held in a relatively new outdoor space, the Bisamberg Lourdes Grotto, built in memory of the original site in France. It was set into the mountain with only the altar and the pulpit protected from rain. The parishioners, mostly women and girls, sat on benches in the open.

As a little girl, I was enthralled by the atmosphere; the mumbled prayers and incantations amid trees and flowers all around. The service was low-key and somehow reassuring. Although, or because, I was baptized Lutheran and did not know the rituals, I was sensitive to the aura of these services with their mixture of mysticism and the everyday. It was a world to which my grandmother unquestioningly belonged and in which I felt warmly at home when I was with her. Sometimes, before or after the service, we walked through the nearby cemetery, and my grandmother told me stories about the people who were buried in the individually decorated graves with their varied gravestones and crosses. She had known many. It was, and still is, considered a shame if a family leaves a grave untended, and she commented approvingly or disapprovingly on the state of certain graves.

My grandmother was superstitious and easily scared, especially by thunderstorms. One time she held me on her lap while we both looked out a window from where we saw lightning strike a house in the distance. It burst into flames, and we watched it burn in horror. Yet, I felt safe with her, and she, perhaps, did the same with me. I was never again afraid of thunderstorms – until I came to the American Midwest.

My mother, I soon sensed, considered the country ways of my grandmother old-fashioned but always showed respect and nursed her as she lay dying from cancer, I believe, although I never heard that word. Despite their living in much closer proximity than my mother had ever imagined they would, I do not recall any arguments between the two women. Only when she was very ill and bedridden did my grandmother complain, mostly to my grandfather and my aunt, who visited every weekend and brought some delicacies for the grandparents to enjoy. However, it was my mother who took care of both her and her sister's parents, which my father never failed to point out. He had little patience and, I believe, felt trapped by having to live in my grandparents' house. It was not the life he had planned, yet after the war, there was no alternative. My parents and grandparents were mutually dependent, we needed a place to stay, and my grandparents needed more and more help. There was no financial support as yet for people like them who had been independent all their lives and owned a house and land. Only when my grandfather was quite old did he receive some pittance from the government. An old-age home was out of the question for either of my grandparents.

Bisamberg by the Danube

Long before us, in the first half of the nineteenth century, Bisamberg, like the other villages to its west, had still been hard to reach from Vienna. However, since 1841, a one-track steam railroad ran from the city to the west and north and stopped in Bisamberg. By my parents' time in the early 20th century, regular train service was a matter of course. It had only one disadvantage, a long walk from the village center to the little wooden station building relatively close to the Danube. Yet old and young, especially the latter, used it to get to the city for school and work. It also served as a matchmaker, as my mother's older sister found when she met her future husband on the daily commute. The last part of the walk, which, depending on where in Bisamberg you came from, took around 30 minutes, went through low-lying fields along a raised footpath with high grassy embankments on both sides and a deep ditch on one, the *Donaugraben.*

Most of the time, this was a tiny rivulet going north, but like all the other smaller and bigger streams belonging to the system of waterways which were part of the Danube, it swelled during the periodic floods which had plagued the area since times immemorial. The more civilization spread, the more disruptive and dangerous these floods became. The high grassy embankments along the *Donaugraben,* which ran very close to my grandparents' house, were man-made and built in the early 20th century as a continuation of the Danube's first major "regulation." Near our house, a monument attested to the inauguration of the *Donaugraben* and the bridge for *Bundesstrasse 1* leading over it. In my grandfather's time, people who wanted extra grass for their rabbits and other animals rented a section of the *Donaugraben* and mowed it; nowadays, the village has it done as part of road maintenance, the embankment providing a pleasant, elevated walk for people and their dogs. I have seen the water rise to the very top of the embankment, but so far, it has never broken through. It would have been a disaster for our house and for the others along our street. When I was a child, there were only a few houses; the rest of the area was covered by small fields. Now all that is built up by ever bigger houses. Apparently, people continue to trust that the *Donaugraben* will hold.

The main street of Bisamberg runs parallel to ours and the *Donaugraben,* but lies higher. Originally, my grandfather owned a house in the safety of the village center and up the mountain, but he sold it to get rid of my grandmother's store and debts on the house. It was not his family's original home, though, as I was told by an old man whom I met during my tutoring visits to various Bisamberg families. When I asked my mother, she had no idea. My grandfather appears to have moved around within the village. He may have sold the house in which he grew up to pay his brother's share of their inheritance, bought another house and store around the time of his marriage, and then sold them after World War I, just when inflation reached its peak, to get rid of the debts he had incurred. If he had waited a bit, all debt would have been wiped out. According to my grandmother, who always regretted this sale, he was lucky to find the smaller house he and then all of us lived in just in time, or his money would have dwindled to nothing. She blamed my grandfather's brother, who worked in a lawyer's office, for bad advice, but I never really knew any details since nobody, but she talked about this. It was one of those family stories about inheritance and money which create bad blood and something my grandfather certainly did not want to discuss, although or because he appears to have come out as the loser. However, he ultimately got what he wished for, independence from any obligations and peace of mind. Again, this is speculation constructed from little bits of information I pieced together out of the occasional remarks my grandmother made, and I remember, although I did not understand them at the time. Even my mother knew nothing, or so it seemed, about the original homestead and never commented on the house in which she had been born.

That house I recall very well, albeit not in its original state, it was close to my grandfather's village vineyard and garden, called "Kirchenweingarten" [church vineyard] on a street named Parkring. This ran above the village and ended at the castle in one direction and the Lourdes Grotto in the other. Most houses there were very nice, as was this one, which we frequently passed when we went to our cellar or the "Kirchenweingarten." I agreed with my grandmother that it was much nicer than the one in which we lived, but I only ever saw it from the outside after it had been remodeled and turned into a little villa with a garden that had all kinds of dwarfs and other nick knacks like tiny castles and trains "embellishing" it. As a small child, I admired that greatly. The house in which my grandfather had grown up no longer existed. According to the old gentleman who told me about it, it had also been in that area, the elevated part in the center of the village.

Now, we lived on the outskirts but were closer to modern transportation. Our little road, as well as the main street of Bisamberg, abutted into the big Highway that led west from Vienna. On its other side, there were fields and an elevated footpath leading to the railroad station. The few houses close to the station always fascinated me because they were a special kind of split level. From the dam to which the footpath widened, small bridges led to their front doors and the upper stories on which people lived. The lower stories and the gardens lay below the dam. Thus, during floods, the owners had dry rooms upstairs. The train tracks and the station were also on embankments, with yet another dam separating them from the side arms of the Danube. Then came still one more embankment of large boulders and a footpath running directly along the Danube in its "regulated" riverbed. All that sounds – and *was* – complex, but as children and young people, we took it for granted as if it had always been that way. Certainly, the forested flood plains stretching to the west had existed "forever" and provided a wonderful wilderness that we enjoyed from early spring through the winter. I remember large drifts of snowdrops in spring, swimming and boating in summer, and skating on the frozen inlets in winter. The Danube itself very rarely froze. If it did, the effects were catastrophic ice dams.

One of The Danube's Many Sidearms

When we were small children, one inlet of the Danube, which lay right beyond the railway station, was still quite large. From the high embankment, you walked down a set of stairs to get to a boat rental with locker rooms. The facility had seen better days but was still run by a ferryman who fit the cliché of being rough and grouchy, certainly with us children. You could rent rowboats from him or be set across the inlet to a small beach. All of it was protected from the Danube by the final embankment. The small beach is where my mother took us bathing in the summer was also where she taught us to swim. Later, we would use our bikes and go on our own. By then, we had graduated to swimming in the Danube proper, spreading our blankets on the grassy spots between the boulders that edged the river. Bathing along the Danube had already been a pastime for our parents and their friends, but not my grandparents and earlier generations in the village.

We returned to Bisamberg in the summers after the War, and from 1950 on, we lived there permanently. Then, we were old enough to roam on our own, and the Danube, its side arms, and the surrounding woods became one of our playgrounds – the Bisamberg being the other. With time, the little side arm where we had learned to swim silted over, but by then, we were no longer interested in it. Our focus was the Danube itself. Across the river on the other side, in the village of Klosterneuburg, a large beach colony and a lido attracted the Viennese proper. Vienna and the surrounding areas then had fewer swimming pools and bathing facilities than now, so in the 1920s, this was a popular spot to go to on weekends because it was easy to reach from the city. Our side was mostly "reserved" for us and the young people who lived in the villages and towns on it. Bridges were far away, so ferries still transported people from one side to the other, as they had done for centuries. The ferryman of our early childhood kept a little motorboat for that purpose, with a bell to summon him from Klosterneuburg. It was rarely used; in general, his business had atrophied. Further upriver, there was a big ferry that could transfer bicycles and even cars as well as people, but we hardly ever went on it. It hung on a cable and was steered into the current, which pulled it across. No motor was needed.

The Danube in our area was a mighty, deep stream with a strong current. The water running through it was quite cold, which was a good thing because you did not notice that it was dirty. Everything, from the waste of the many river barges to that from smaller abutting communities and houses, went into the "Blue Danube." Yet, because of the current, the depth, and the cold temperature, all you smelled occasionally was an oil slick which you could see as well. Although I had a very sensitive nose, I never thought about pollution – which must have been much worse below Vienna. Now, things have been cleaned up, and downriver from the city, there is a large Nature Park.

As small children, we were warned about the river's dangerous eddies, which made it all the more exciting to us as young teenagers. We then made a sport out of swimming across, something our father had first done with us. It took the better part of a summer afternoon.

We walked upstream and swam diagonally against the current as hard as possible so we wouldn't drift downriver too far. On the other side, we explored the lido a bit, walked up again, and returned. To make the swim more exciting, my brother liked to cross in front of one of the many barges and ships that traveled up and down the Danube. We knew full well that we could be sucked under if we came too close to them, but my brother loved to skirt danger, and, scared as I was, I went along, so we would not drift too far apart.

We turned up our noses at the activities in the lido on the other side, such as minigolf, and, more to the point, we did not have any money on us anyway. Besides, we much preferred our "uncivilized" side and our more strenuous activities. Another favorite form of entertainment was watching out for passing ships and gauging how big their waves would be. If the waves were of a promising size, we ran upstream, jumped in, and let them carry us far down. Occasionally convoys of small Russian battleships passed by and produced the largest, most wonderful waves. Austria was still occupied, with our part of the Danube in Russian hands. The battleships looked like toy boats from afar, but close-up, they were daunting in their grey solidity, which only added to their fascination. We, certainly I, did not reflect on their role nor on our closeness to the Iron Curtain.

We took the wide river, the elaborate dam structures, and the extensive wooded areas with their many small waterways on our side of the Danube for granted. I only learned later that much of that was the result of the first major "regulation" of the Danube between 1870-1875, which was meant to save Vienna and surrounding areas from the frequent and ever more devastating floods. Earlier attempts at taming this major European waterway, the only big one that runs from West to East through the center of the continent, had not been successful. Then, in the 19th century, the floods and their devastation in parts of Vienna and the communities along the river's paths and how to "regulate" them became a much-debated priority. "Regulation" was finally undertaken. Thus, the much beloved

Danube as we knew it in our childhood and our teenage years had not been there "forever." It was the creation of engineers and a company that had also built the Suez Canal. Around Vienna, it cut a new riverbed some distance from the center city but left the arm, which had previously served as a major waterway, as the *Donaukanal*. Another part of the old river system around Vienna was turned into a recreation area called the *Alte Donau* [the Old Danube], with boat rentals and baths. Upriver, in the direction of Bisamberg, large open flood plains were created, and still further upstream, the woods and little waterways next to the bolder-encased Danube proper, where we spent our summers as children and young people, continued to stretch west. We did not know or care that our "wild" paradise was partly the result of the first Danube "regulation," nor did we expect that things would change again.

Yet they did. Despite its enormous scope, this first "regulation" was not enough, and so, in the nineteen seventies, years after I had left home, another major flood project was undertaken. I saw its effects when I came for visits: Our "wild" playground was gone, and a four-lane highway into Vienna had been built. It was protected by floodgates that could be quickly shut. Further upstream, there was even a wall all along the road going west which could be raised to keep floods at bay. So far, all that has held.

The new highway makes access to Vienna fast and easy. As a student, it took me one hour to get to the University by public transportation; now, it takes 15 minutes by car. The little rail line has also been upgraded, offering well-protected, fast service downtown. Further upriver from Bisamberg, however, the old towns and villages such as Dürnstein or Melk, parts of which had been built close to the water, are still affected and, almost proudly, display flood markers going back for centuries. The abbey of Melk, however, had always been safe. It holds a commanding position on a high outcropping of rock – the medieval monks had known what to do. A footpath on the dam along the river all the way from Vienna to Passau on the German border, which already existed in my childhood and youth and goes back to the Middle Ages, is still there, now paved for walking and biking. Some of the woods and flooded areas also still exist in places, but much of it is gone. The core of the village of Bisamberg, which wisely clung to the mountain, was never directly affected, but all fields around it and the lower-lying houses like ours had always been in danger, even if, as children and young adults, we never thought about it. I wonder if our parents or grandparents did.

People in Bisamberg

When I lived in Bisamberg, it had been relatively accessible to Vienna proper for some time, a fact which had transformed its population to a mix of country and city folk. The differences in attitudes, lifestyles, and aspirations between my mother and grandmother were characteristic of the place in general and left their imprint on me and my brothers. Farmers and vintners were still an important population, but increasingly, people from the city or oriented towards the city lived there as well – seasonally or long-term. There were the summer people who came for what the Viennese called "Sommerfrische" [literally: summer freshness]. They did so to a much larger degree on the other side of the Danube in the Vienna Woods, but our little mountain attracted its share.

Summers in the city were not pleasant, and those who could, tried to spend them in the rural outskirts. Beethoven is a famous and early example. The aristocracy had had their summer palaces for centuries, some far away on their estates in Hungary or Bohemia, some quite close, such as the Emperors' *Schönbrunn* and Prince Eugen of Savoy's *Belvedere* or the Liechtensteins' winter and summer residences, which are in walking distance of each other. Now, these summer palaces are surrounded by the city but retain small or large parks and gardens. In the later nineteenth and early twentieth centuries, ordinary people of some wealth, like my uncle's father, also bought or built, if not castles, then villas on the fringes of Vienna, in Bisamberg or, more frequently, in the readily accessible villages of the Vienna Woods.

Others of some means who could not, or would not, invest that much money in a house, rented rooms with local people who vacated parts of theirs. When my mother was a young woman, my grandparents sublet their largest room to a couple who came every year and brought their maid along. She prepared meals in the kitchen and must have slept there as well. According to my mother, who considered this fact amusing, she never waited to eat the leftovers but had her meals before her employers. Their son and his girl became close friends with my parents, and my mother, who was still living at home, learned quite a few traditional Viennese recipes from madam and maid. She admired the young couple and their happy-go-lucky attitude and told me approvingly that when the friend wanted to go out in the evening but not stop at home, he simply bought a new shirt and changed into it in a telephone booth. This couple lost everything in the War except their *joie de vivre* and stayed friends with my parents. Growing up, I came to know and like them as well.

Many upper-middle-class Viennese also went further away, into the mountains and lake regions of the Alps, such as Bad Aussee or Bad Ischl. Emperor Francis Joseph, who had a summer villa in Bad Ischl and loved to go hunting there and everywhere, served as a model. Still, a lot of ordinary people, middle class and up, preferred the immediate, rural, and pretty environs of the city because husbands could work in Vienna during the week and join their families on weekends; a few even commuted. Our little village had quite a few inns with shady gardens where locals, mostly the men and summer folk, gathered in the evenings. I know from hearsay that my grandfather went occasionally and drew attention as the attractive man he was. I do not believe my grandmother ever came along, though. One favorite entertainment was bowling nine pins, with the better establishments providing old-fashioned bowling alleys and hiring boys to set up the pins. World War II ended all that for good, and I never saw a bowling alley in use, only the dilapidated remains. Still, when I was growing up, there were a few inns left, and now there are none. Bisamberg had yet another group of "city folks" living there who were year-round residents because it was cheaper and/or healthier for the children. The breadwinners went back and forth every day and all year, were retired, or had independent incomes. This group became more prevalent in the period between the two wars.

My Zehl-Grandfather

My father's family belonged to that group. My Zehl-grandfather was a railroad official in the Austro-Hungarian Empire and stationmaster in Brünn (Brno) when the Empire collapsed. Civil servants and German families were then repatriated, and my grandfather apparently oversaw the orderly evacuation from Brno. Family lore has it that he held up a whole train of evacuees so that my grandmother, ever the good housewife, and mother, could run to the market to buy a few geese. The ones in Brno were better than those in Vienna and cheaper.

Zehl Grandfather

I do not know if my grandfather, like so many German-speaking civil servants of the Empire, continued working for the much-diminished railroad system that was left to serve tiny Austria after the Monarchy's dissolution or if he was pensioned off, but as far as I understand none of those civil servants were simply let go. I remember my grandfather sitting at what to me seemed a very large dining table in their apartment in a 19th-century villa in Bisamberg, and not just for meals. It was his spot. He was Lutheran and a presbyter in the small Lutheran church of Korneuburg, the next town over. This grandfather came from a family with roots in Germany and Bohemia. As far as our records go back, all his forebears had worked as officials for local or imperial governments. Family lore also has it that my grandfather loved books so much that his purchases threatened to bankrupt the family. Consequently, his practical and resolute wife had his salary – or pension – garnished. Another related hobby of his was bookbinding. By the time we were back in Bisamberg for good, we had inherited his library, which among other books and periodicals, contained volume after volume of the journal *Der getreue Eckhart* [*Faithful Eckhart*], beautifully bound by my grandfather. Its orientation was German Nationalist, something I understood only much later. As a young teenager, I loved looking through the journal and enjoyed the stories, the fashions, and the frequent sections on interior design, which reminded me of our apartment in Vienna and its furnishings. They must have served as an inspiration to my parents, especially my mother.

I only knew my Zehl, or Linz-grandfather as we called him, when I was a small child. I remember running to meet him when he came down our little street, a friendly old man who dressed formally and liked to smoke cigars. His daughter, my aunt, married somebody from Linz, where her wealthy in-laws owned a large photography shop and an even larger apartment house. When her husband, Uncle Willy, joined the *Wehrmacht,* she began to help in the shop developing pictures. My grandmother then moved from Bisamberg to Linz so she could help with my aunt's three small children and took my grandfather along. She lived for her children and grandchildren and, much later, even insisted on keeping house for my cousins when they were students in Vienna and had a small apartment there.

I do not know, but I cannot help wondering what role my grandfather played for my grandmother in his last years. I am sure she took good care of him, but he does not appear to have been her priority. At some point during the war, he had a stroke and became bedridden. When there were bombing raids – Linz had major industries, most notably the Hermann-Göring-Werke, as they were called then (now VOEST), and attracted many – my grandmother took her grandchildren to the basement for shelter but could not move my grandfather from the third floor where they all lived. There was no elevator. A bomb destroyed the top part of the house while he lay in his bed against the one wall that did not collapse. He died in early 1945. I only know all that from stories and always wondered what went through my grandfather's mind when everything exploded around him.

My Linz-Grandmother

It was my mother who told me these stories; my grandmother said nothing in all the years I knew and spent time with her. The few reminiscences she shared had to do with her as a young woman. She liked to recall that on Sundays, her family used to go out to a coffee house or inn, that she wore a new blouse every time, and that she had quite a few suitors. She did not say why she had chosen grandfather; he certainly had been a good, steady "prospect," and she was a very capable woman who wanted to be a housewife and mother.

Did she later regret her choice? I do not think so, but her unwavering support belonged to her daughter, granddaughters, and daughters-in-law. She came from Vienna and had grown up in the city, the only one in our family. When I knew her, she was a stately and always well-kept woman, although she rarely went out except to visit family, including her third set of three grandchildren who also lived in Bisamberg. Her youngest son, my uncle Fromund or Mundl, of whom I have no clear recollection, died right after the War, supposedly for lack of penicillin. My father and my aunt wanted as little as possible to do with his widow and her mother. There was illegitimacy, but I do not know the details and don't believe that this was the reason they kept their distance. I gleaned that they thought my uncle had been trapped by mother and daughter, who were a bit strange and lived in an illusionary world, which they probably had to do, isolated and poor as they were, although my aunt's father supposedly was a well-off dentist. My grandmother visited them regularly, though, and I enjoyed going with her. The household was very different from ours and somewhat chaotic, which I found interesting. There were two unruly male cousins who were slightly younger than I and difficult for the women to manage, as well as an older sister who had a hard time with them and about whom my grandmother was especially worried. Indeed, she was concerned about the future of all three of those grandchildren.

As it turns out, they did well. The oldest son was materially the most successful because he married into a trucking business, enlarged it, and broadcast the name Zehl on his lorries all over the area, the younger and wilder one learned to be a skilled craftsman, and the girl became a goldsmith, I believe, and married a stable, slightly older man. The couple, who had no children, later visited with us and was well received by my father. My grandmother could feel relieved and content.

She had a reasonably large pension but did not use much of it for herself because, since she had moved in with my aunt, she never owned nor wanted a place of her own. Thus, besides paying for her clothes and small needs, she apportioned most of her pension for presents for her children and nine grandchildren, for birthdays and

Christmases. I do not know if she occasionally supported her dead son's family as well. After we had moved back to Bisamberg, she and my Linz cousins spent summers with us for a number of years. She helped in any way she could, cooking, putting up preserves, etc. Sometimes, we were six children and five adults in a relatively small house. For us children, it was great fun. My brother and I, as well as my male cousin, were allowed to sleep in bunkbeds in the unfinished attic next to a large window looking out on a walnut tree that was larger than the house. We loved it. My mother appreciated her mother-in-law and the fact that she never interfered. Later, my grandmother was also understanding of my teenage needs. When I was around sixteen, e.g., there was a dance in Korneuburg, which I badly wanted to attend but for which my father demanded a chaperone. Neither he nor my mother would take me, but my grandmother did. Afterward, we had about an hour's walk back home. One of my dance partners came along, but for someone like her who had trouble with their legs, it turned out to be a bit much.

Proud Zehl Grandmother, with Klaus and Horst

Sadly, none of us could help her when, much later, she fell over one of the ubiquitous little oriental rugs at my aunt's and broke her hip – a hip which had probably been in bad shape for some time. As far as I know, there were no operations or hip replacements available then. My mother went to Linz to care for my grandmother but could not stay, and neither she nor my aunt could lift or handle the elderly woman. Thus, my grandmother remained bedridden for the rest of her life and had to be put into a nursing home. It was a good one, and we all visited as often as we could.

At the time, I was already in the US, but when I came to Austria, I always went to see her and, at one point, brought my baby son to show her her first great-grandchild. However, she was more excited to hear that my brother had just graduated with an advanced engineering degree. Ours was the generation she had lived with and for. On special occasions, such as but not only significant birthdays, she was put in a wheelchair and brought to my aunt's apartment, where we had a family party for her. However, for long days, months, and years, she lived in a room with three other old bedridden women. She remained alert and never complained, at least not to me, but she waited more and more impatiently for the morphine she received every afternoon. Knowing all the treatment that is available nowadays, I wonder if more could not have been done then, but I trust that my aunt and my parents explored all options. Still, it was not the end this active and loving woman deserved.

Family Birthday Party for Grandmother in Linz, including her brother, standing on left.

Our Parents

When my mother left the Vienna apartment, there was no question that she would move back in with her father and mother, temporarily as they all thought. In many ways, it was a good arrangement. My Bisamberg grandmother served as a built-in babysitter, which allowed my mother quite a bit of freedom of movement. For all practical purposes, she, like so many women at the time, was a single mother, but with the advantages of a support structure and a good income. She was secure – if not safe – and independent at the same time. Of course, I am sure she missed my father and, in the end, was luckier than many women because he returned. Did she then feel a loss of control? I do not think so. My father clearly took charge again, and she did everything to keep him happy. At the time, concepts like post-traumatic stress disorder were not in use, but my mother understood that the man who came back was damaged by the war, even if it took quite some time for the effects to manifest themselves. On an everyday level, she continued to make decisions and took care of all the mundane tasks which my father considered demeaning, and there were quite a few. He had spent the war in commanding positions and in very different circumstances.

Yet, he was a dedicated family man and did his best for us, getting work immediately when he returned from the war and building a new career. She appreciated his reliability and care and stressed them, even as she suffered under his increasingly frequent bad moods. These developed only later, though, for as he grew older gastric problems and emphysema made life harder for him, and his tendency to self-medicate did not help. Besides, disappointment may have also played a role: It took much longer to establish himself again to some prominence than his original joy at surviving, and his still youthful vigor and optimism had led him to believe. He was only sixty-two when he died after a second stroke. My mother then talked about missing him very much, did not accept a marriage proposal she received, and never mentioned the stresses she had had to bear as they grew older. We, and I believe I can say "we," loved our father very much, as children and as young adults, and appreciated his obvious dedication to the family. But later, we also saw his weaknesses and emotionally sided with our mother, whom

83

we respected very much. Thanks to her, there were "only" outbursts on my father's part but never any fights.

However, in their younger years, my parents even enjoyed two "honeymoons," neither of which was the traditional after-the-wedding kind. Then there was not much time. My father needed to return to the unit he had just joined. But when, in early 1939, soon after my brother's birth, my father and other officers in the Austrian army were called to Berlin for training and integration into the *Wehrmacht*, my mother joined him. He, like his comrades, except for one who supposedly refused to leave Austria, did not hesitate. On the contrary, with his Lutheran upbringing and his family's Germanic background, he was, I believe, eager to become part of the bigger country with its sizable Lutheran population and a large army. It meant a widening of his horizons and prospects. Besides, he had little choice.

I do not know how aware he was that war was imminent, but he must have had a good idea. He had become a professional soldier and was proud of it. As such, he should have expected to go to war, although he did not and could not know what lay ahead. As catastrophic as World War I had been, especially for Austria, Hitler's war, its reasons, circumstances, and consequences represented yet another dimension of disaster and destruction, physical and moral, which demanded more foresight than my father, or my mother, had at the time. It is easy for me to look back and wonder what they were thinking. Did they really expect that the Third Reich would win whatever wars it got into and then carry on peacefully? Afterward, I never heard my parents mention Hitler, and I never asked what they thought of him then or had thought of him earlier.

However, when my father was called to Berlin, and my mother joined him there, life appeared promising. They were still young and without worries – we children were with the grandparents. For my mother, it was a wonderful, free, and easy time in THE modern city. She rented rooms, liked her landlady, visited the sights, and went out with my father and other young couples. Unlike so much else she did not talk about, she enjoyed telling me about her stay in Berlin, which she remembered fondly and in complete disassociation from what came later. This short interlude, along with the apartment in Vienna, gave her a brief taste of the life which she had expected to lead. The second "honeymoon" was very different; it came at the War's end when my father returned. They had survived and were together again. For the moment, that was more than enough. My younger brother arrived in March of 1947.

The Cinema Next-Door

Waiting for her life to start in full, my mother enjoyed her wartime existence in Bisamberg as best she could. At least, that is the impression I had as a child and carry with me. In the country cinema right next door to us, she had her reserved seat where she met her women friends and saw every new film with my brother and me being safe and secure with our grandparents. This cinema was a little gem. When I attended it as a young teenager, it was already in decline. However, for a few years, my brother and I could still enjoy it as well, even if the films screened then were mostly uninspired postwar Austrian productions or old Nazi films deemed inoffensive. The cinema's entrance was on the main street, which ran parallel to the small road on which we lived but was higher up. The cinema had been specially built as such, as had been many similar establishments in the villages and small towns everywhere around. During the War, it screened all the films an active Nazi industry distributed, including the newsreels, which provided enough propaganda so that the features could be somewhat less obvious in their message. Indeed, quite a few of these movies, mostly forgettable comedies, and romances, were still shown long after the war had ended. I do not remember any of the films I saw, but I do recall that many of the postwar ones were set in the Alps and dealt with an evil poacher, a good hunter/gamekeeper, and a lovely Austrian-style cowgirl or innkeeper's daughter. Many of the actors stayed with me, though. Their careers continued without interruption from the Third Reich into postwar Austria, such as those of Hans Moser, Paula Wessely, Paul, and, Attila Hörbiger, etc.

Some of these actors had already been well-known before the "Anschluss" and starred in theaters as well as films, with their careers proceeding rather seamlessly, while those who were Jewish had to leave. For the most part, they did not return, even if actors found it harder than directors to get work elsewhere. The famous film *The Third Man,* set in postwar Vienna, is interesting in that respect because its British director brought together returnees as well as those who had stayed on, with actors from Britain and the US. However, this kind of collaboration was rare, and ultimately, the Austrians and Germans who had stayed had the upper hand, and newcomers started out.

As you do nowadays in many European cities, you had to walk down into our little cinema. But here, the double, pseudo-baroque staircase was outdoors. It started at street level with display cases on each side and a concession stand next to one, the owner's house next to the other. The lobby where you bought tickets was downstairs. From there, you proceeded to a screening room which was at the level of our road. The projection booth was in a little tower dominating the front of this rather ornate building, not a film palace but a tiny film castle. The screening room was quite large, at least in my memory. It had doors all along one side serving as security exits and were often opened for fresh air. If you stepped outside, you found yourself in the owner's orchard, which ran along our garden and house. In case of fire, you could safely exit onto our road. As young teenagers, my brother and I went home that way. We were never brazen enough, though, to try to sneak in without going through the lobby and buying tickets, although, by then, the cinema was not full anymore.

Neighbors

Besides her love of cinema, which she gave up completely after the War, my mother enjoyed playing cards. She often visited an elderly lady down the road, Tante Emma we called her when we came along to feed her canary with pieces of sugar. We did not stay long; the card games did not interest us. But when my mother played solitaire at home, I loved sitting next to her and watching. Soon, I knew many of her games, all of which I have again forgotten. Much later, she would continue the tradition by teaching various card games to my children.

Another elderly lady my brother and I visited frequently was our next-door neighbor. She was very friendly with my grandparents and my mother and liked children. There was a small window in our fence – all houses and gardens were and still are fenced-in – through which you could communicate and pass things without going around from house to house. We had no telephone; perhaps this neighbor did. Her household was more "modern" than my grandparents' in many little ways. She had running water, a modern toilet, and, I believe, a bathroom; we did not. I noticed those differences but cannot say that the lack of such conveniences bothered us children. What interested me were the games and books our neighbor had. During the Hitler period, her husband was the region's "Gauleiter" [head of the local NSDAP = Nationalsozialistische Deutsche Aurbeiterpartei]; I do not know what he had done before nor what became of him afterward. We never saw him. I also do not remember any Nazi insignia around her house, but would I have noticed? Our neighbor had a large, well-maintained garden and let us play wherever we wanted and pick whatever fruit we wished, which was not the usual behavior of people her age and time. Her sons were long grown, one had been a fighter pilot and been shot down, but I am not sure when. On my walks through the cemetery with my grandmother, I admired his grave, which stood out in its sleek, futurismo monumentality of dark marble.

The other son worked for the GESTAPO (Secret Police) but was never around. I do not think my grandparents or my mother were aware of what he did then or where he went after the War – to prison, into hiding? Much later on, he appeared and moved into his mother's house, which he had inherited. Then, he tried to establish neighborly relations, but my parents wanted nothing to do with him. I do not remember what happened to his mother; we left Bisamberg before the War ended and when we came back, she was gone. I believe I asked about her but do not recall the response.

The Neighbor Nextdoor with my Brother and Me (in the background)

Immediately after the War, the neighbor's house was in the hands of squatters. That period was more chaotic in the Russian-occupied areas of Austria than in the US sector, where we had found refuge. Vienna, like Berlin, was divided up into four zones, and Bisamberg – as well as Lower Austria – was in Russian hands. For a short time, personal retribution and looting by Austrians were common in these areas. All of it could be blamed on the "Russians."

When we started visiting my grandparents during summers, probably in 1947 or 1948, we found a large Bisamberg family of ill repute next door. They had been living in a shack at the foot of a quarry we passed when we went to our grandfather's vineyard. I became friends with one of the sons, who was a bit older and a "bad boy" type, which began to interest and attract me. He bragged openly that he and his siblings stole much more than the Russians who got the blame. When we moved to Bisamberg for good in 1950, he and his family were already gone from the neighbor's house. I do not know what became of this "friend."

Under the immediate postwar circumstances, old and single women like Tante Emma suffered greatly. She was a genteel lady and had been kind to everybody, but nobody was there to look out for her. My mother was gone. She told me later that right at the end of the war, Tante Emma, whose house had been bombed, was seen on a stretcher, reaching out an emaciated hand begging for a boiled potato. That image stayed with me, although I never saw it myself. It was my grandmother who gave her that potato, but she could not follow up on what happened with Tante Emma. My grandparents were old as well and had Russians occupy their house, but they were country people like many of the soldiers and let be. They knew better than to resist and managed, as many in the village did and had done for centuries under occupying armies.

Mother during the War

During most of the war, we lived quite comfortably, there was enough food, and my mother had more than enough money. My parents invested some of it in a campaign by Volkswagen, where you regularly bought stamps and glued them into a booklet. When full, it would entitle you to a Volkswagen. My parents' little book was almost full when I found it long after the War. In many ways, my mother's life was on hold, and in hindsight, she lived on borrowed time. Again, it is hard for me today to imagine what future she expected. Did she really believe that Hitler would win the War and then her life with my father would take off? How long did she hold on to what hopes? She knew she had married a professional soldier, which included separation in war. But during peacetime, families could be together. Until the end of the Third Reich and the revelations about its atrocities, which took time to seep into the consciousness of the general population, being an officer in the military was considered an honorable, even prestigious, profession.

World War I had not substantially changed this centuries-old perception. And now, it holds again in Germany as well as in Austria, albeit diminished. As the War progressed and the situation became more dire, my mother may no longer have allowed herself to think or worry at all beyond our day-to-day existence, which continued in the accustomed surroundings of her parents' house. To us children, she appeared calm. Curious as I was as a little girl about the conversations of adults, I did not catch any concerns, but she probably did not voice her worries when we were around. As for myself, I believed the slogan "Wir werden siegen" [We will win], which I clearly remember seeing scrawled on trucks and walls everywhere, but I had no idea of its meaning.

My mother's decisions were made on her own. She probably shared them in letters to my father but, understandably, could not always wait for a response. They concentrated on our well-being and survival in the moment and, in hindsight, were as good as possible. These included decisions like moving us out of the city back to Bisamberg and eventually fleeing west, ahead of the Russian army. After the war, she never talked about all of that, and I did not ask the questions I should have, sensing that she did not want to answer. She became defensive whenever I came close to anything touching upon the Third Reich. One time, I did wonder why my father had joined the training in Berlin, a stupid question anyway. She was clearly upset and responded, somewhat huffily, "Of course, he did. All the others but one joined as well. What should he have done?"

I believe that she did enjoy being a young mother, and as such, did not only have the support of her parents and rural traditions but also of Nazi propaganda about motherhood. She contributed to the household by helping in the gardens, doing much of the cooking, which was simple country fare, and, first and foremost, taking excellent care of me and my brother, who was only fifteen months younger. Without any so-called modern conveniences, all that kept her very busy. In a letter she wrote to me many years later, she mentioned how much work it had been. This was not, as she said, to complain or to praise herself but to allay my brother's concerns about a second child and how hard that would be for his wife. She told me things had become so much easier and she was glad for her daughter-in-law.

Everyday Life for Us Children

Even in our rural surroundings, it was important to my mother that we be well dressed, which was fine with fastidious little me. Not only did I enjoy a bow in my hair and the nice clothes my mother made for me, but I also became easily disgusted by many aspects of country life, such as pigs, chicken droppings, and critters like worms and pill bugs. My brother and I were very close, but he still loved to "gross me out," especially with those pill bugs he found everywhere. However, the most repugnant incident, which totally disturbed my dainty equilibrium and which I cannot forget, was of my own doing. Dressed up in a coat I loved, I waited in the yard to go out. To while away the time, I balanced around the concrete rim of my grandfather's manure pit, which had recently been emptied. I promptly stumbled and fell into the slurry at the bottom. It was a catastrophe, although, thankfully, I was not physically hurt. Of course, in hindsight, it was much worse for my poor mother, who had to clean me up, no easy task, and comfort me, which was even harder. I was so extremely distraught.

We had some friends in Bisamberg and many second cousins, but we did not play that much with other children except with a slightly older girl who lived right across the street. With her, we did gymnastics on the grass right between our houses. This road, which is now lined with cars, was still unpaved and had no traffic. In general, my brother and I were enough for each other. Besides, our mother spent a lot of time with us. When I was still quite small – it may have been my third birthday – I received the most wonderful present, a bike my father sent from Belgium, where he was stationed at the beginning of the War. He also sent Belgian chocolates, but to make them last longer, my mother kept them in the cellar since we had no refrigerator. They eventually became covered by a white film, which made them seem unappetizing to me. Otherwise, they would have been a special treat. There was no candy available, as far as I remember. What I do recall are the empty chocolate and candy automats at train and tram stations, though, and my fantasizing about how wonderful it would be if I threw some money in and got a wrapped piece of something sweet to come out. The idea appealed to me more than my longing for sweets; we had enough homemade treats like cookies, cakes, and "Mehlspeisen" [dishes made with flour as a main ingredient and mostly sweet] in general.

The bike, however, was my joy and pride. No child had one – producing children's bikes was not essential to the war effort. It was green and had no brakes whatsoever. When I wanted to stop, I put my feet on the ground and scraped to a halt. Downhill, I stretched my legs away and let it run. I shared it and still remember that some second cousins, who were very popular, learned to ride it on the village's main street with all the children cheering them on. I felt a bit of an outsider then, a feeling that probably correctly reflected my place in the village. It was a feeling I never quite lost wherever I went. However, this did not usually bother me, and when I was a child, I considered it a badge of honor to not quite belong – or at least that is what I told myself. I certainly did not want to join all the little Catholic girls in the village who had their first communion and got their ears pierced to put on the customary present of a set of earrings.

Bikes became our general mode of transportation, at first with my brother sitting in a basket fixed to the handlebars of my mother's. Thus, we could easily get to our relatively far-flung destinations, such as the Danube and my grandparents' gardens. One time, my habit of rattling down a steep dirt road with outstretched legs ended in a spectacular fall. Not unusual for Austrians, a passerby scolded my mother quite vehemently for not watching me more carefully. She, however, was not worried and trusted my brother and me to do what we thought we could, scraped knees or not.

With My Bike.

She did make sure, however, that we learned to swim early on, probably because she herself was not a good swimmer. I was four when she taught me in the side arm of the Danube, where we often went bathing. She held me up by my braids as she showed me. How she taught my scrappy brother, on the other hand, I do not remember, perhaps with a belt we had, which was made of cork pieces and helped keep him afloat. Even as a little kid, my brother was a daredevil, and I, the elder sibling, usually followed him if physical courage was demanded, but I remained squeamish. He never was and soon learned to do practical things that I would not do, such as feed the pigs and milk the goats which my grandparents kept. The pigs frightened me with their grunting and their shoving at feeding time. You had to open the trapdoor to their trough, which swung to the inside, to pour their slop, but I was afraid the pigs' shoving would push it towards me and allow them to get out and have a go at me. Still, I did enjoy living in the country. We spent much of our time in my grandparents' gardens and vineyards. There were trees to climb, flowers and grasses to collect, and fruit to pick. My grandfather knew all the plants and trees, of course, and my mother, many.

Our vineyard, with its wonderful views, was on one side of the Bisamberg; the other big garden was near the village church and looked down upon it. There was also a large field along the road to the next village. Why were my grandfather's properties so far apart? I never asked myself that question, but it probably had to do with century-old inheritance and purchase whenever there was a chance. Land was and is valuable, especially in the environs of Vienna.

Excursions

We enjoyed our rural lives, but my mother made sure we did not become total country bumpkins and took us on periodic outings to the city before and after we lived there. On these special occasions, which often occurred when the family from Linz came to visit, we frequently went to the Natural History Museum, one of the two big museums facing each other on the Ringstraße. The second was dedicated to Art History, but we never went to it, perhaps because my mother thought we were too young, although it might have excited me more. The Natural History Museum, with its large rooms full of endless glass cases of stones and fossils, oozed boredom to me from the minute we entered. By the time we would come upon some potentially more interesting exhibits, I was tired.

Family Outing with my Grandfather, Aunt and Cousin from Linz

Another outing that I did not appreciate, although I did not complain – it was an outing, after all – was the Schönbrunn Zoo. It was the former Imperial Zoo and is still one of Vienna's major attractions. The reason I did not like it lay right at the entrance. There both sides were lined with baroque pavilions, which contained wolves and perhaps other wild animals. The poor creatures paced up and down, up and down in those cramped spaces. I felt so sorry for them that I was immediately turned off the whole visit. Nowadays, there is a different entrance, the pavilions are empty, and the wolves have some open space to roam; still, these early visits made me dislike zoos, even if I later took my grandchildren.

One childhood outing I really loved, though, was a visit to the Diana bath and pool complex. When we lived in Vienna, it was relatively close to our apartment, but we also made a few trips from Bisamberg. At that time, there was no pool anywhere close. The Dianabad saw several incarnations and no longer exists, but the one I knew was the pinnacle of early 20th-century bathing sophistication. I admired it when I was a little girl and later when I was a student at the university. On entering the lobby, you were greeted by the smell of water, steam, and perfume from the hairdresser and other stores that opened into it. In the center, there was a fountain with a statue of a boy riding a dolphin. The Dianabad had many floors below street level, which were a world of their own, with steam baths, saunas, and small pools of ice cold to very hot water, with massage rooms and rooms for resting. The basins were tiled with mosaics in fin-de-siècle imitation of Roman baths. I went down there once with my mother and returned many times when I was a student. As a child, I was excited by the many floors that were above ground, with entire balconies of dressing rooms surrounding a large pool. The higher up our dressing room was, the scarier it became to look down upon the pool, which then appeared quite small. There was even a 10-meter diving board, but I never saw anybody use it. The Dianabad had a smaller pool as well, which we were particularly fond of because there was a slide. It was very modest in comparison to today's elaborate ones but new and exciting to my brother and me. Every half an hour, this pool produced large waves, another wonderful rarity. To me, Dianabad was heaven on earth.

Books

In winter and for long summer evenings, there were always books. I recall only a few picture books. One was a collection of benign children's rhymes with pastel drawings; the others, much less benign, were *Max und Moritz*, a very early comic with verse, and the famous/infamous *Struwelpeter*. The first repelled me by the evil pranks Max and Moritz played on people, who struck me as not very likable either, as well as the horrible end they come to: ground in a mill to kernels on which chicken feed. The second, had a series of equally harsh punishments for mostly minor transgressions like not eating one's soup, leading to starvation indicated by a grave. The image that really frightened me, though, was the one that is still relevant today. It features an enormous man picking up two kids who have made fun of a black child and dunking them into a gigantic inkwell. I did not appreciate the Brothers Grimms' fairy tales either because I thought that they ended badly. Of course, they do not, but for me, the characters' tribulations must have overshadowed any happy ending. Besides, in German the last words are often ironic and playful: "Und wenn sie nicht gestorben sind, dann leben sie heute noch." [And if they did not die, then they are still alive today.] Perhaps that was not satisfying enough.

I loved the collections of Greek and Norse legends which were simplified and sanitized for children, but we must have encountered those a bit later when we could read well enough ourselves. For me, this came around age 7, and from then on, I devoured what seems like every book for young people that existed, and there were many. All through my childhood and youth, books were steady companions. I remember quite a few of them vividly and much better than the ones I read now. Relatively early on, but surely after the War, we came across the three-part series *Die Höhlenkinder* [The Cave Children]. It told about a boy and a girl who find themselves suddenly alone and completely cut off from other humans. To survive, they go through the stages of early civilizations, from cave dwellings to a hut on stilts in the water and eventually to a stone house, all in the period of one young life span. Eventually, they have a baby, although there is no explanation of how they go about producing it. It is made clear from the very beginning, however, that they are not brother and sister. The books end with the little family finding a way out of their hidden valley.

We also loved the many volumes by the quintessential German writer Karl May, who is still being read today, albeit much less than before. They were passed on from one generation to the next and, long after the War, were turned into popular movies with German actors playing Native Americans. By then, though, our enthusiasm, which lasted well into our later teenage years, had waned. In his books, Karl May was the hero of his own stories, either as Old Shatterhand among the Indians, as he and we called Native Americans then, in the US or as a distinguished traveler in the Middle East. When he wrote his books, he had not been to either part of the world; it was all his fantasy. We gleefully and proudly recited the long name of his faithful Arab servant, who was presented as a funny character with the then customary condescension towards "others."

In the US stories, however, Old Shatterhand has a close friend, the noble chief of the Apaches, Winnetou, whose story May tells in three volumes. I refused to read the third because I knew Winnetou would die in it. In the books, he and his fellow Apaches are treated with great respect and as equals; there is no condescension there. On the contrary, they were "noble savages," actually a kind of "other" as well. To my surprise, I learned later that in the US, the Apaches are often typecast as treacherous Natives, and the Sioux, the villains in the German author's books, are the "good" ones.

A very different book we loved was *Der Kampf um Rom* (The Fight for Rome) by the 19th-century nationalist lawyer and popular historian Felix Dahn. We read him at a time when he should have already disappeared from bookshelves, but he was beloved by fathers and uncles – and by us. We did not know enough to be discriminating and enjoyed all kinds of stories. Thank goodness, growing up, we soon found books that counterbalanced the heavy Germanophile and nationalist influences which still abounded, but I will return to that. In fact, much of the reading I mention here happened a bit later as well, when I was about eight and older, and we briefly lived in Linz. One book I never found in my family's collection was Hitler's *Mein Kampf,* perhaps nobody bothered, or it was quickly thrown out at the end of the War, but by whom? My parents were not in Bisamberg then. As a child and young teenager, I never even knew that this book existed.

Flight: Wesenufer

In early 1945, there must have been many warnings about the dangers the approaching Russian army posed for women and children. Was there advice that they should flee? I do not know, but one day, my brother and I found ourselves on a train full of other children and their mothers heading west. Again, I remember excitement but not fear. We had a clear destination, Linz, where my aunt and my Linz-grandmother lived. However, once there, we found only the in-laws' maid – I do not know where the in-laws were – and the information that my aunt and grandmother had moved even further west to Wesenufer, a little village on the Danube near Passau and the German border. We had vacationed there together a few years earlier, of which I have no recollection, only some photographs. My aunt likely sought refuge in this out-of-the-way place to escape the constant bombing raids on Linz, which had already destroyed her apartment. She and my grandmother were probably less worried about the approaching Russian army, although it did come close enough, eventually stopping north of the Danube and east at the River Enns on the border between Upper and Lower Austria.

Earlier Vacation in Wesenufer, probably 1943

During our overnight stay in Linz, a major bombing raid drove us into our first and last big bomb shelter expressly built for that purpose, an enormous bunker dug into the mountain there and equipped for sleeping. When we came out the next morning, my mother picked up the two suitcases with which she had left Bisamberg, only to find, much later, that they were the wrong ones. Judging from the content, they had belonged to a young woman without children. There was no way to return or exchange them. I do not know when my mother realized her mistake, perhaps only after she had arrived in Wesenufer. She certainly held on to them all the way, probably nervous and worried enough not to notice what had happened. However, with us children, she kept a calm and confident front as we made our increasingly difficult trek from Linz to Wesenufer, first by train, then by hitchhiking, and finally by walking. Only much later, in a rare admission, did she tell me how exhausted and close to a breakdown she had been by then. I vividly remember walking on a lonely road through a dark forest at night, with my mother carrying those two suitcases and my brother and me holding on to each side. Yet, I was not scared, nor did my brother appear to be. He was barely six. Whatever desperation my mother felt, she communicated calm and certainty to us. When we came to the farmhouse and the one room in which my grandmother, my aunt, and her three children stayed, my aunt opened the door, embraced my mother, and said, "Thank God you are here." My mother never forgot this welcome, even if my aunt's self-assured and seemingly arrogant ways sometimes irritated or hurt her.

Women and Children at Wesenufer Farm

During the day, the three women and five children lived in this one room. I do not know if they cooked there as well or in the farm's kitchen. This farm consisted of a few more women of different generations and many children around our ages – from three to eight. It was spring, so we could all play outside. There were no men. The first men we saw were the American soldiers who slowly drove through the village in their open jeeps and threw candy at us. I do not know how long we had been in Wesenufer before they came, but it cannot have been long.

To relieve the crowding at the small farmhouse, my mother looked for a place for the three of us to sleep and found a tiny room with two single beds against each wall and a narrow space in between. It was in a gamekeeper's cottage in the large forest that stretched all along both sides of the Danube. The man was old and bedridden, but had a kindly housekeeper who gave us milk and potatoes when we arrived in the evening. My mother used the skin on the milk as a butter substitute to roast the potatoes. When the housekeeper made real butter in an old wooden churner, a process I loved to watch, she gave us a little as well. It was so-called country butter, soft, watery, and incredibly delicious – something you later could buy at farmers' markets. The gamekeeper was, or had been, employed on a large estate which, as far as I know, consisted of forest and stretched far across the Danube into Bohemia. The Russians now occupied the northern side of the river, and the owners had fled quickly from wherever they had lived, probably in one of the many castles in Bohemia. I heard they had a blockhouse built close to their gamekeeper's stone cottage, but I never knew who they were and never saw anybody. We, children, were probably told to stay out of the way – perhaps the gamekeeper should not have taken us in, to begin with – but nobody bothered us.

On our berry-picking forages through the forest, we did encounter a much more fascinating, and indeed, mythic figure, though, a "Köhler" [charcoal burner], who appears in many a German fairy tale. Ours was very real, sitting next to his tent-like pile of wood pieces in which he tended a slow-burning fire. I think he lived right there as well. At the time, his presence in the woods appeared normal to me. He was all sooty and looked scary but was quite friendly. A question I ask myself now is, "Had he been there throughout the War?"

When we walked to our sleeping quarters in the evening – it was quite far – we took a path along the Danube. Since the Russians were on the other side of the river, US soldiers had quickly erected little guardhouses along its banks. The young men were kind to us children and invited us into their tiny huts to give us packets of Hershey chocolate which they had opened to the silver wrappers and melted on a potbelly stove. It was still cool at night. My brother and I enjoyed these chocolates as wonderful delicacies, although now I turn up my nose at Hershey chocolates. At the time, though, any kind of sweet was something rare and special, but we never went hungry. My mother, aunt, and grandmother were enterprising and resourceful women, which we, five children, with me being the oldest, took for granted. My aunt and mother went as far as Linz, almost 50 kilometers, on bikes, which they must have borrowed, to check on things there and scour for food. As spring advanced, my brother, cousin, and I helped pick berries, wild strawberries, raspberries, and, finally, blueberries. We also collected the new growth on the tips of fir tree branches. They were then boiled to produce a honey-like syrup which we spread on bread. It was a fragrant treat. The adults were quite strict about us children eating as balanced a meal as they could produce. I still do not like beets because I had to eat beet sauce before I could get some of the cherry strudel I badly wanted.

In the summer of 1945, my father returned from his POW Camp in Germany. Among the papers my mother left me there was this short note dated July 24 which tells her that he had been released and was on the way home, i. e. to Linz and his mother and sister. He did not say anything about Bisamberg or Vienna. Perhaps the last thing he had heard was that my mother planned to head for Linz, or, more likely, he was wary of the situation in the Russian-occupied areas. Social media, of course, did not exist then, and telephones rarely worked, but word-of-mouth did, and returning soldiers, even if the other allies had correctly released them, were afraid of ending up in Siberia as happened to their comrades whom the Russians took as prisoners of war. My father's note is brief and impersonal so that everybody can see it. Was it the first message my mother received after the letters from East Prussia? The fact that she kept and passed it on may suggest that. On the other hand, I would assume that the POW Camp allowed inmates to write home, which my father would have done, but to Bisamberg, where this note might have gone initially as well.

What my father told us later: In his camp, exclusively for officers, they had all been treated well, and he had been assigned some administrative duties which involved checking release papers. When he saw what reasons were acceptable, he used similar ones to get himself out as well. My father did not stay with us in Wesenufer, though, but he immediately looked for work to support us. The money my parents had in the bank was worthless. At first, you could not buy anything with it, then in November of 1945, there was a currency reform. It allowed people to exchange no more than 150 Reichsmark into the equivalent in Schillings, Austria's money during the First Republic, which was being reinstated as our currency and lasted until the Euro came in 1999. I do not know what my father's military pay had been, but whatever my parents had saved – it was probably quite a bit – was lost.

My father quickly found employment, though, and according to later contracts I saw, earned between 200 and 300 Schillings which apparently was quite enough. His job, on an agreement from September 15, 1945, was "Lagerführer" [camp director/manager] of first one and then, another, Camp for Displaced Persons. The DPs I met were people who had come in treks from the East and were housed in former barracks. They soon moved out and established themselves, usually quite successfully. At least, that is what I observed around Linz and Bisamberg.

 Much later, I read about the horrible conditions for DPs in Germany. But as a child, I saw none of that and gleaned nothing from the conversations I overheard. The camps in Austria served the people who had come west along the Danube and had been craftsmen, professionals, or well-to-do farmers. As I already mentioned, their flight was less chaotic than what happened farther north. Displaced and at first probably still hoping to return, they soon settled down to stay, and, rather quickly, built new lives for themselves, at least the ones I encountered as I grew up. They realized that there was no chance of returning, nor did they want to. In Austria, they exerted much less pressure on politics than they did for many years in Germany. The areas they came from had not been part of Austria for a long time, if ever. Thus, there was no pressure to dispute the new eastern borders decided upon after WWII, as there was in Germany.

In his position, my father needed staff. So, among others, he hired my uncle and a friend, who both feared returning to Vienna. My uncle had good reasons. Since he had been a Nazi, his and his father's business in Vienna was – briefly – confiscated. His wife, my aunt, stayed behind to hold on to their claims and what property she could. Singlehandedly, she faced the repercussions for her father-in-law's and her husband's political stance – hers never came up for discussion – as happened so often. Soon though, my uncle could, and did, return to Vienna. For a while, they all had to accept a co-owner in their business and many inhabitants in their Bisamberg villa, but eventually, they returned to full possession of the stores. It took longer to gain complete use of the villa again in Bisamberg simply because there was a housing shortage, and they had an apartment in the city. I only knew my uncle as a kindly, somewhat fussy older man and had no idea about his political past. It was my younger brother who mentioned it many years later. He was ten years my junior and much better informed than I was about these matters because, during his youth, the silence about Austria's Nazi past slowly began to crack.

In Linz

We did not leave Wesenufer right when my father returned. The women and children stayed there for the rest of the summer, and he came to visit on weekends. Then he would bring rare delicacies such as fresh rolls and cold cuts. I assume he shared his bounty with the rest of the family, but I fondly recall that, in the evenings, it became special family time for the four of us. We put a board between the beds in our tiny room and had a feast. My parents' pleasure in being together again – it was their second "honeymoon" – and our enjoyment in having a father eclipsed everything else, even the good food. Still, with the cold season approaching, we could not stay in our primitive and crowded surroundings, although they never bothered us children. It was difficult to find housing in Linz, which had suffered significant damage from the bombing raids. Apparently, my father did not wish to move us into the camp he administered, or he was not allowed to, possibly an indication that things there were not quite as good as my childish impressions led me to believe. At any rate, he always considered his job temporary and wanted longer-lasting lodgings for us. Thus, the larger family came to an arrangement that suited us all: When my aunt's apartment had been destroyed by a bomb, she had been assigned housing close by in somebody else's large apartment. That was Third Reich procedure, I understand. Why she was not given space at the time in her in-laws' even bigger place, I do not know. Only the top floor of their house had been destroyed. The rest, including their apartment below, was safely intact and protected from collapse or rain.

When their son, my uncle Willy, his mother's pride and joy, returned from the war soon after my father, his parents decided to make room for him. Then, my grandmother, my aunt, uncle, and three cousins moved in with them but maintained separate households. We received the place they had originally been assigned. The owners of that apartment could not, or did not, object, although they were not happy with our presence. We children rarely saw them but were told to be quiet when we came in and out through the large hallway and used the shared toilet, which, in Austria, is normally separate from the bathroom. The family had two adult daughters, the younger one became friends with my parents, especially my father, but otherwise, there was no contact.

The set-up in our aunt's and our places was similar, with theirs a bit larger because it had a live-in verandah, but in both apartments, the bathrooms were turned into kitchens, probably because they had water and some connection for a cooking stove. We had two small rooms, both with windows to the back garden. One was our living/dining room with a large couch where my parents slept; the other contained bunk beds and – when our little brother was born - a crib. Under the window, my father constructed a double desk for my brother and me to do our homework and keep the few toys and the books we collected. Our room opened into the former bathroom which had a stove for cooking, a sink, and – over the bathtub – a large board for meal preparation. There was a cabinet above. Thus, bathing for us was a complicated affair and impossible for our landlords. In this makeshift kitchen, my mother prepared meals for four people and bath water and baby food for my little brother. There was also the danger of mixing up toiletries from over the lavatory with cooking ingredients, such as one time when brilliantine was used for "Knödel" [dumplings] instead of oil. The apartment was quite cramped, yet I experienced it as comfortable and cozy. Occasionally we even hosted overnight visitors, such as my grandfather from Bisamberg, who slept on the bottom bunk while my brother and I shared the top.

Once, my father's cousins, two couples who lived in Upper Austria, stayed for a night. Then our "living room" became one big makeshift bed, a fun event for us children. Every Saturday evening, my Uncle Harry, my father's friend, and my Linz aunt and uncle gathered in our parents' tiny apartment to visit and chat. It was fun for us children to have these guests, even if we had to go to bed early. We vicariously experienced the adults' joy at being alive and together, and I listened to their animated murmurs right next door until I fell asleep.

Saturday Evenings in Linz: Uncle Willy, Father, Mother, Uncle Harry

I also loved to visit my father in his camps. The first one was in old-fashioned brick buildings, the second in one-floor wooden barracks. In both, I was treated like a little VIP. All the people I encountered, mostly women, were kind to me. I saw fascinating things, especially textiles, and ceramics, they had brought with them and met interesting people. What intrigued me most was the way many of the country women dressed. They wore lots of skirts, one over the other, with one of them being a white lacy one showing just a little bit on the bottom. On the days they did the wash, the different skirts hung on long lines and provided a gaiety their owners probably did not feel. When I later read Günter Grass' *Tin Drum*, I instantly recognized his description of Oscar's grandmother and her skirts. Not all the inhabitants of the camps were country people, though. My father made friends with a couple who were both doctors. They served us tea in their rooms, which were decorated with colorful rugs and struck me as a beautiful oasis in the hustle and bustle around them. I had no sense of their losses and did not remember their talking about them. Indeed, none of the adults I encountered spoke about the past and what they had lost. Perhaps I was just childishly insensitive and did not listen well enough, or perhaps they were careful about what they said in front of my father or me. And surely, they wanted to look forward, not backward.

My father had a truck at his disposal for the camp's business. Normally, my uncle, a motorcycle and car enthusiast, served as chauffeur for the camp, but on weekends, my father could use the truck for himself, which meant for us. The whole family, including my aunt, my cousins, and soon, my baby brother, in his carriage, were piled onto it for outings. I remember St. Florian, the beautiful baroque monastery associated with the composer Anton Bruckner, of whom there was much talk and a little music when we visited the place, which we did quite frequently. More important for us, as children, was the river Traun nearby. It is a little stream and, coming from the mountains, the water that runs through it is quite cold. In the large inundation area along its sides – the river swells up considerably in spring when the snow melts – there were small pools and beaches for bathing and picnicking.

My father, who always wanted a challenge for my brother and me, took us swimming in the Traun itself, which had a very fast current. Despite my trepidations, I came along, and of course, my brother did, too; our cousin was more hesitant. We were around eight and nine then. When I saw the Traun much later, from the train or road going by, I was surprised at how small it was in normal times, but as a child, it appeared daunting to me, even in summer.

We also used the truck for a trip into the Alps to visit my uncle Harry's sister and her teenage children, who had found refuge near the famous *Krimmler Falls*. It was my first experience of the high Alps, and I was immediately and forever captivated by their stunning beauty. As usual, my father was not very cautious and drove into remote valleys on paths that were quite narrow and not safe for the truck. We had no accidents, though, except later in Linz when another driver ran into us, and those on the bed of the truck got thrown about. At the time, there were no laws against transporting people, including children and baby carriages, the way

109

we did. Driving around in the Alps, we encountered little traffic and saw few other tourists – if any. All this made the experience incomparable with any later excursions when, hiking or skiing, I always felt that there were too many people everywhere, even in out-of-the-way places.

Visiting in the Alps, Uncle Harry, Mother, Klaus, Father, myself, my Uncle's Sister and her Children

That same summer – it must have been 1946 – we had another wonderful vacation in the Alps. Mother, aunt, grandmother, and five children went to a large inn at the entrance to the Gosau lakes at the foot of the Dachstein, where my Linz uncle (Willy) had connections through his family's photography and postcard business. The inn's owner likely wanted to have new pictures taken to start things up again. As yet, there were very few people at the inn, and we probably paid little but had the run of the place. I vaguely remember that we children could choose our own bedrooms and even switch them. From some rooms, you could climb out of the window and be on the hillside behind. In the late afternoons, when we came home from swimming, my grandmother served us all the fresh country bread she had bought in the village, with marmalade, in the inn's dining room. Lunch was less memorable, but there was always soup.

My father came to visit and took the three of us, my brother, my cousin, and me on an overnight tour into the high mountains to a hut from where serious climbers started their ascent onto the Dachstein and its glaciers. We were the only children there and quite proud of ourselves since we had clambered up some steep paths and rocks to get there. We also admired the men – there were no women – who, in the late afternoon, sat outside the hut, on boulders with their sore feet soaking in basins of water; they were some of the first "tourists" we encountered. Apparently, climbers had never completely stopped coming – mountaineering was always big in Austria, before, during, and after the Nazis, but it was not yet the enormous industry it is now. We, the children, enjoyed that my father took us to interesting and challenging places.

Three Mountaineers

The Dachstein with one of the Gosau Lakes

I also vividly remember a trip the whole family made with the truck to Hallstatt, a village perched on the mountainside over a lake named after it. Its beauty and its macabre aura impressed me deeply. The lake was dark because the surrounding high mountains allowed little sunshine to fall on it. It struck me as foreboding. In addition, the place proudly displayed its ossuary full of skulls and bones which went back for centuries. We were told that the village was so old and had so little space that graves could not be allowed to last. Hallstatt's age and fame had to do with its ancient salt mines, which we also visited. There is even a period in prehistoric times named after Hallstatt, a fact which fascinated me because it opened new vistas, e.g. that long ago people had traded and traveled through this difficult-to-reach place and that lowly, everyday salt was so important. There are many towns and villages in the area with Hall, which refers to salt, in their names, but Hallstatt, with its hard-to-reach and, therefore, safe location, had been the most significant.

Since then, I am always interested in anything I hear or read about Celts, these still mysterious early inhabitants of Hallstatt and Europe. Exiting in a different way was the fact that my father insisted on driving into Hallstatt through the narrow town gate and almost got stuck. We had to get out to check that he did not do any damage to the gate or truck. Parking and making it back out were other worries. Nowadays, he would not be allowed anywhere near Hallstatt in a truck or car. It is seriously overcrowded by tourists – even on foot.

The following year, we went to another part of the massive Dachstein range, this time by train, and hiked five hours up to its famous Ice Caves. Again, there were no children our age in the hut, where we slept in a big room next to many others. These were wonderful trips and were only possible many years ago. Now, a cable car goes up to the caves, as well as the top of the Dachstein, where an observation deck of glass makes the stunning beauty of this area accessible to many people as effortlessly as possible. For that reason, I never sought to go back there; I did not want to damage my early memories, which included some sense of having earned the enjoyment of all this beauty and the illusion that it was there only for those who had worked for it. Yet I used every occasion to hike or ski elsewhere in the Alps, often with my brother. Besides becoming an excellent skier, he also became a serious mountaineer and climber. It's safe to say that our early experiences formed us deeply.

On the Gosau trip, I also had a less-than-wonderful experience which did not really spoil my stay, though, but which I could not forget either. One time, all of us were packing up from bathing by the lake nearest our inn. Except for us, nobody else seemed to be there. I was dawdling when suddenly a man appeared from behind one of the neat stacks of wood that were piled up everywhere along mountain roads. He said he wanted to show me something, and, always curious, I stayed behind the others who probably had not even noticed him. I do not recall if he undressed in front of me, but to my surprise and disgust, he suddenly stood there naked and masturbating. I had no idea what he was doing, but I saw these white, little worms come from his penis. I was grossed out at the sight and immediately ran after my family. He did not stop me. I must have been embarrassed about the incident because I did not tell anybody about it. I also stayed close to my family for the next few days but did not see the man again.

The only other experience of the kind that little girls – and boys – sadly sometimes have, was quite different. It was in Linz, and I was on the way home with my brother when an American soldier followed us to our apartment, where my parents let him in. They thought he was a lonely young man and talked with him. My father knew English. The soldier came back a few times, bringing things like coffee, chocolates, and eggs, which he wanted my mother to scramble for him. Usually, my brother and I went to bed before he left, but he always came into our room and wanted a kiss from me, which I refused to give him. My parents laughed at his attempts, and he never tried to catch me by myself, of which there was little chance anyway. Still, I was wary, although nobody else seemed to be.

We lived in Linz from the fall of 1945 to 1950, but at some point, we children and my mother began spending part of our summers in Bisamberg, where my mother helped her parents with their gardens. Besides, fresh air was the family mantra, even if we were not exactly shut up in Linz either. To be sure, there we lived in the center of town in an upper-middle-class area on a street that was appropriately called Bürgerstraße [Burgherstreet]. However, the two or three-story houses which lined it all had gardens in the back. They usually belonged to the owners who lived on one floor while renting out the rest. This was the case with our house as well. Our rooms were on the mezzanine, while the homeowner, a lawyer for Opel, I believe, had the whole floor above us. There was still another family on the third floor whom we never saw. The owner had children, a daughter, and two sons.

One son was close in age to us and became our playmate. There also was a cousin who had moved in with his mother from Germany. Briefly, another family with a slightly older girl stayed there as well. She and I never became friends because she wanted nothing to do with the boys and preferred showing off using her beautiful clothes and stories of who she was. I liked playing with boys and had only one close girlfriend when we lived in Linz. Her mother offended mine, though, when she claimed that some scissors we used for cutting out dresses to fit onto paper dolls were really hers. After that incident, I stopped seeing the girl, but I did not miss our playdates. The boys were more fun anyway.

Like most of the houses in the neighborhood, "ours" had a little paved yard with a contraption for beating rugs right off the back door. It was enclosed and accessible to everybody, but the garden beyond, although not locked, was reserved for the owner. It became our playground even though it was not designed for children, except for a small corner with a swing set we never used. The rest was a garden typical of the later 19th and early twentieth centuries, with gravel walks and stones encasing the flower and rose beds. At my aunt's (or rather her in-laws') house, up the same street, there was a similar garden which we also turned into a playground, this time with our cousins.

Both gardens were the worse for wear after we left, although we tried to be somewhat careful of the flower beds. The garden in the back of "our" house had a small pond with goldfish, a gazebo, and a rockery with the ubiquitous woodlice/pill bugs under its stones. Now three boys were chasing me with them. At my aunt's, there were enough of those critters as well, but I was the oldest and, thus, a bit of an "authority" figure. Instead of a gazebo, this house had a large verandah to shelter us from rain and allow us to continue playing. All this sounds and was idyllic, yet our few-minute walk from one place to the other took us past one or two bombed-out houses, which were part of our world as well. We took it all in stride, although I occasionally wondered if there would ever be houses again instead of these ruins.

Sometimes, my brother and I even stopped at one and clambered around where dandelions and little trees had begun to sprout. There was nothing keeping us out, although it was probably not very safe. Even at my aunt's, where the staircase to the bombed-out third floor was shut off, my brother went up and looked around in the rubble. Both my aunt's and our houses had balconies that opened to the gardens, so adults could keep an eye on the children. At "our" house, the cousin from Germany was a crybaby, an invitation to the other two boys to tease him even more. When he got upset, he ran to the area under the balcony and called his aunt. "Tante Thea, Tante Thea!" I can still hear him. Although I did not participate in the taunts, I did not defend him either and did not like him very much.

The house had a basement apartment as well where refugees from the East lived. They had children approximately our age, but we did not invite them to play with us, nor did they ever ask. It never entered my mind that we were refugees as well, but, apparently, a different class and "only" internally displaced; everybody treated my father with respect and us as equals.

I do not recall how my brother and I divided our time. At first, we may have spent more of it with our cousins, where my grandmother could keep an eye on us while my mother was in the latter stages of her pregnancy and then had our baby brother to take care of. I was nine going on ten years then but had no understanding of pregnancy and was unhappy that my mother became so "fat." During that time, my brother broke his leg playing soccer and continued to do so with his cast, which he also broke. This upset my normally calm grandmother very much, but we had no idea why. We did not understand that she had her hands full with all of us. My mother's pregnancy was not easy, and my aunt had to worry about her husband, who was very ill and died soon thereafter. I comprehended very little of this because we were shielded from everything deemed inappropriate for children.

Mother with my Baby Brother Richard

Before my baby brother came home, we only saw him once when a nurse showed him to us in the hallway of the hospital, all swaddled in white lace, as was the custom. Nothing but his tiny head showed, which was quite misshapen, as our friend from upstairs, who came along, remarked quite loudly. I was upset with him for speaking out, but also with the fact. As I learned later, it had not only been a difficult pregnancy but also a difficult birth, and my mother needed time to recover. When she finally came home with the baby, I immediately fell in love with him. Bathing him in our small apartment, which was done every day, was quite a procedure. We used a little wooden bathtub for which we heated water on our stove. It had to be just right. Drying, powdering, and dressing was done on a stack of blankets and towels on our dining room table. Soon, I knew how to do all this by myself and enjoyed being in charge. My female cousins sometimes came to watch. What I did not have to do, I now know but never thought about at the time, was wash all his clothes and diapers. There were no pampers, of course. My mother had almost no help; only the woman from the basement assisted with the washing.

Bathing Putzi, with Cousins Watching

With Putzi

When my little brother, whom we called Putzi [*putzig* means cute], was a few months old, I began taking him to the nearby park and made such a fuss over him that one time when my father came along, two old women wondered if I was the mother. He laughed; I was proud. I remember paying a lot of attention to my baby brother, but in the scheme of things, it probably was not that much because, besides school, we continued to spend a lot of time with our upstairs friends and our cousins. As the oldest of the cousins, I directed activities among them playing school with me as the teacher. I prepared lesson booklets with the letters of the alphabet drawn carefully and scenes and words which used them. We even had a blackboard. My female cousins, who were three and five years younger, had to sit in little chairs and pay attention. We also held theater performances with a blanket suspended between trees serving as a curtain, but I do not remember what we performed.

Theater in the Garden.

In our house, I was the only girl. The boys, especially the cousin from Germany, were keen on playing Adam and Eve in the basement, which essentially meant undressing. I felt very uncomfortable and nixed that "game" quickly. In the gazebo and in our friends' upstairs apartment, we engaged in endless card and board games. We had many so-called "Quartett" games, which are similar to *Go Fish* but more "educational." In these games, individual players must collect as many sets of four cards as they can. Depending on the game, the categories were rivers, cities, countries, flowers, composers, etc., and had subsets within those categories, such as tributaries to the Danube.

Among the board games, our favorite was Parchesi. I do not remember playing chess, probably because there were too many of us. One game we were not excited about was Monopoly. We had a version called DKT which used Austrian capitals, with Vienna containing the most expensive real estate, but the game took too long and struck us as boring. None of us was a budding businessman/woman.

For communication at night, my brother, who was already interested in electronics – he would become a successful electrical engineer and work on major international projects – built a separate telephone line to the room above ours so we could talk at night while hiding under our duvets. Our friend's father was so impressed that he once called our father on it. We also came up with less constructive entertainment: When everybody upstairs was out, we went into the father's study, which, together with the salon next door, served as his office during the day and had a telephone. There, we looked up random names in the directory, and then one of us dialed the number. When somebody on the other end answered, we banged the table, even popped light bulbs on the street below, and cried for help. After that, we hung up. We were lucky that the apartment was rarely empty, so we had few occasions to play this "game" and did not get caught.

By then, my father had left his job as camp administrator, which had probably run its course, and had begun working as an electrical engineer for which he had studied as a young man before he had joined the Austrian army. There was no more truck to take us places, but on weekends when my mother stayed home with the baby, we took the train for outings further away. There were many. We went hiking, skiing, and searching for mushrooms. I did not like to eat mushrooms then, but hunting for them was great fun. My father taught us to identify the edible ones. Chanterelles were good, but the prized ones were in the Boletus family, "Herrenpilze" and "Steinpilze." "Fliegenpilze" [toadstools] were to be avoided, which was easy enough. We set out with a big box in our rucksack and sometimes came back with only a few pieces banging around in it. At other times, we had a haul which my mother and grandmother turned into a mushroom sauce with "Knödel" or, alternatively, into

122

breaded and fried mushroom slices with potato salad. For the adults, these were delicacies. I only ate the "Knödel" or the potato salad. Stomping around the large forests north of the Danube was magical, though. You could leave any path and roam freely because there was no underbrush, unlike the U.S., where it is difficult to wander freely in the woods I know. We never got lost on our mushroom-hunting expeditions – thanks to my father.

Somewhere in these forests, by a small gorge, there was also a little house that belonged to my aunt's in-laws. It could only be reached on foot and perhaps by cart and had no electricity or running water, but there was a brook right next to it. I do not remember if we stopped there with my father, probably not, but we children, including our cousins of course, spent some time there with our grandmother. It was a great adventure for us, probably less so for her, but she was always game and shared my aunt's and mother's views that children needed lots of fresh air, preferably unpolluted by a city like Linz with its heavy industry, which was being built up again. I am pretty sure none of the adults knew that, not far from our idyllic house in the woods, there was Mauthausen, Austria's notorious concentration camp. I do not recall ever hearing it mentioned when I lived in Linz, nor later as a student in Vienna.

My Aunt Inge became a widow around 1947/48 and went back to work in her in-laws' flourishing photography business, mostly developing pictures. Perhaps, she had never stopped. I liked to visit her in her darkroom and "help," but it must have been lonely and boring work for her. From my child's perspective and probably in reality, her in-laws were not particularly nice to her. At least, she and my grandmother made remarks along those lines. However, everything was *comme il faut*, my cousins could hold their birthday parties in the in-laws' large living room, and I was allowed to practice on their grand piano there, even if we rarely saw them. But on the 6th of December, St. Nikolaus' Day in Austria, the grandfather dressed up as bishop St. Nick and came with a sack full of nuts, apples, and sweets, accompanied by the maid as the popular

"Knecht Ruprecht" or "Krampus," a kind of devil, with a chain and a switch to frighten children into being good.

Birthday Party "comme il faut"

Yet, the business, in which my aunt worked until her retirement, was passed on to a grandson who had shown no interest until then, not to my aunt or her son. However, to be fair, my cousin was not interested anyway. He wanted to study theology.

Tante Inge with Her 3 Children

As a widow, his mother was a very attractive woman and had many admirers whom she juggled as best she could. Some were married, and she became friends with their wives as well. I vaguely remember one couple where the man was the new director of VOEST, still or again the dominant industry in Linz, and the wife was a stout woman next to whom my aunt looked particularly glamorous. Her bond with this couple and others was Bridge, which she played until she died in her early nineties. One admirer was single, though, Uncle Karl, whom we children saw often. He was the main "boyfriend," who ate at my aunt's table frequently and supported the household financially, but he never moved in or stayed overnight.

According to my grandmother, my aunt would have liked for him to marry her, but he claimed to be a confirmed bachelor. He changed his mind only when he advanced in age, but then my aunt was no longer interested. I have no idea what his background was, and I don't think he had been a soldier. At the time, he was a salesman for the digestive, Underberg, whose little green bottles were stocked by every restaurant and bar. This meant he was financially well off.

I did not care for him nor did my father, who put up with him because he loved his sister. My cousins probably also had reservations about Uncle Karl, especially as they grew older. Only my younger brother liked him because when he visited my aunt in Linz, he was invited to come along on sales trips around Upper Austria.

He was the youngest of us all, impressionable, and seemed to be without our reservations against salesmen, which were, of course, snobbish. However, I believe, coming from a long line of civil servants, my father had reservations not only against salesmen but even my solid businessmen uncles. Much later, I heard Uncle Karl had moved into the same nursing home where my grandmother had been – and hanged himself there. I have no idea if by then my aunt had broken up with him, if she had ever really loved him, which is hard for me to imagine, or if she just felt she had to have a man in her life. After the war, single men his age were rare.

Looking back, I realize that she managed very well on her own. My three cousins went to university. Horst became a minister and moved to Germany, where he did social work. Liese and Evi stayed in Vienna. Liese went into education and eventually became a *Hofrätin* – by then, the coveted title was conferred on women too. Evi was a lawyer. Eventually, my aunt moved to Vienna as well, where she followed in my grandmother's footsteps by taking care of her grandchildren after school. However, she had her own apartment, and the children came there. She also found a circle of Bridge players in downtown Vienna where she became a regular.

To me, my aunt appeared a formidable woman, superbly competent and beautiful. When I was a little girl, I enjoyed sneaking into her bedroom and rummaging through her dressing table with its many lipsticks, nail polishes, and perfumes. My mother did not use cosmetics and even considered nail polish vulgar but excused it on my aunt because the chemicals used for developing photos discolored the nails. At least, that is what she told me. Into old age,

126

Tante Inge remained a very attractive and well-groomed woman. I admired her and still do, but now mostly for bringing up her children as a single mother and doing it well. To be sure, she had my grandmother, who was fiercely loyal to her daughter and always supported her.

After Putzi's birth in 1947, my brother and I needed and received little supervision. It must have been at Christmas that year when our major gifts were bikes. I remember being a little disappointed at the paucity of presents that year. Perhaps my brother felt the same. This made our surprise even more exciting. As we sat down to our traditional Christmas Eve dinner of fried fish and potato salad, my father sent us to the basement to get some wine, and there they were, two bicycles, a brand-new one and a refurbished one. We did not care which was which; we were elated. The bikes increased our range considerably. At first, we polished them after every ride, which made our friends from upstairs laugh at us. Our enthusiasm for cleaning would not last, they said, and they were right, but our enjoyment of and need for bikes stayed with us into young adulthood. In fact, it even increased when we moved back to Bisamberg.

I must have been around twelve when the older brother upstairs, who had never joined our games, took notice of me and became my "Verehrer" [admirer], an old-fashioned word for boyfriend, which does not carry quite the same meaning though, because theoretically, the girl makes no commitment, she is just being wooed. He was three years older than I and went to the *Humanistisches Gymnasium*, which still taught Greek as well as Latin and was only for boys. By then, I went to the all-girls *Realgymnasium*, which also prepared me for university study but taught English and Latin. I must have had some afternoon classes because when he began his "courtship," he waited for me in the dusk.

We walked along a secluded path, held hands, and exchanged secrets. He told me that his father expected him to become a lawyer to carry on the business, but he wanted to study medicine. When I met him a few years later, on a visit to Linz, he had become a law student. That was the last time I saw him or heard of him. He gave me my first kiss – on the cheek. I enjoyed our secret walks and the atmosphere around us. In the following summer, when he appeared pale compared to the boys in the *Parkbad,* I was less interested in him. His sport was fencing which did appeal to me and which I wanted to learn, but, as my father reasoned – he had also done fencing as a young man – I should not try because my eyesight wasn't good enough. It was a classy sport but not one that made you look bronzed and attractive, which seemed important to me when we went swimming. Among all the boys I spent time with in the coming years, he was the most reputable, yet ultimately the most uninteresting to me. I was more drawn to the ones who were a bit "wilder."

In school, I was a good student. Only one of my teachers did not like me at all, perhaps because the others did. Too bad it was the music teacher and choir mistress. Despite my mother's efforts at having me take piano lessons to improve my ear for music, it quickly became obvious to that teacher that I had no talent and could not carry a tune. In Austria, this is a serious deficiency; at least I experienced it as such, perhaps because of that teacher, even though I liked music and later tried to compensate for my bad ear by studying music history. Instead of ignoring my deficiencies as many future instructors did, this one enjoyed humiliating me in front of the whole class by demanding that I sing a certain note, such as an "A," which, of course, I could not do. Completely unrelated to my lack of musical abilities, she grabbed my hands and accused me of biting my nails in front of everybody. It was something I never did.

One year, when the school planned its Christmas party, the German teacher selected me to recite the introductory poem because I liked poetry and could do it well. However, the music teacher, who

128

directed the event, which was mostly about her choir performing Christmas carols, did not want me to participate. To my disappointment, the German teacher did not stand up for me. Still, this incident and the teacher, while they spoiled a particular event and every bit of confidence in my musical abilities, did not affect me enough to make me dislike school. I enjoyed going and felt it was good to me. I was the one child chosen to be sent to England on an exchange, which was really a one-sided invitation, a charitable endeavor on the part of the British for war-torn Austria, even though England itself had suffered considerably, as I realized when I was there. We were a group of boys and girls of around eleven whose first great adventure was the ferry across the channel; none of us had traveled much or at all. The boat's crew set out a beautiful tea for us with molded jello in bright colors decorating each plate. I had never seen nor eaten jello and was impressed by the elegance – briefly – then I became violently sick. I was not the only one.

Upon our arrival, we were first bused to a castle in Lancashire. It was early spring and beautifully green everywhere, with stone walls and borders full of daffodils. I fell in love with England then and there. After two weeks in the castle, we were distributed among families, two sets, each for three weeks. I and another girl, who became my friend, were sent to Blackpool, a popular seaside resort. My first family was very nice, even if the household struck me as quite untidy. I found out later that the lady of the house would have liked me to help her a bit, but I had no idea of this then, and she did not say anything. Tea was my favorite meal, with little cakes or muffins every time. At Easter, I received the biggest chocolate egg I have ever seen. I also had my first fish and chips wrapped in newspaper, which I still love, although I do not get it in the newspaper anymore.

The second family ran a bed-and-breakfast very close to the sea. Looking back, I believe the first family was solid British middle class, while the second was originally working class. At the time, I found the latter more relaxed and their house nicer. After all, it was set up for receiving guests. During vacations and on weekends, it was full, and we children – there were a few – had to sleep in nooks and crannies. Otherwise, we could choose our bedrooms. The family came from Preston, an industrial town nearby. One time they took me along for a visit to relatives. All of them were friendly and kind, but I had to be careful not to let on how shocked I was by the grime I encountered everywhere. The streets and, even more so, the back alleys which ran behind the miserable little rowhouses, were sooty and ugly. Thank goodness, the bed-and-breakfast in Blackpool was quite different and not only close to the beach but also to the boardwalk and a complex called Fun House. My Austrian friend and I loved going there and trying out the various activities. You had to pay for some, but quite often, people, mostly men, gave us the money to participate. None of them ever bothered us, though, and we never thought anybody would. We had a wonderful time, but I soon lost contact with my host families, which was my fault. Besides a thank you, I did not manage to establish a real correspondence. Thus, they never learned how important and formative this stay in England would be to my life and how much gratitude I owed them, but then I did not know either.

When I was back in school, the English teacher asked me to speak to the class about my experiences, in English, of course, only to be told afterward by my classmates that I sounded terribly affected. I had acquired a British accent without being aware of it and kept it until I had lived in the US for a while. At the time, it was the right accent to have in Austria, but my classmates were not accustomed to it, probably because our English teacher did not have one either. So far, she had not had a chance to go to England and must have had a strong Austrian accent – which is quite different, by the way, from a German one.

Besides the impression that England made, there was the America House in Linz which exerted considerable American influence on me. My brother and I went there regularly for books – in German translation. The America House had a large selection of books for young people that exposed us to a whole different world from the German nationalist literature, which still filled the bookcases we had access to. We did not know enough to make a clear distinction, but we loved reading and devoured everything we could get. I very much enjoyed finding out about different countries and the lives of young people in these countries. I also liked the style of most of these books, which I found less ponderous and more approachable. Not all the books were translations of American stories. There were many from Scandinavian countries and some from Switzerland, like the *Swiss Family Robinson*. I do not know if the America House had the famous *Heidi* books – I certainly never read them, nor did I ever want to; from what I had heard, they were sentimental and sugary, too much so for my taste. However, I fondly remember translations from Norwegian literature about a girl my age who spent her summers in Spitzbergen among reindeer herders. Some of the American books I remember include *Leatherstocking Tales* and *The Last of the Mohicans* by Fenimore Cooper, which were a bit heavier and slower going. They painted a very different picture of Native Americans and life on the frontier than our beloved Karl May. The America House was modeled on what I would later admire, the US Public Library. It was open, welcoming, and comfortable. Lending libraries existed in Austria as well, but they were not so widespread and not so accessible, certainly not to children. I do not recall ever going to one.

In the America House, we could also see subtitled films for young people. They were black and white and enjoyable, but that is all I recall. Nobody pushed my brother or me to the America House. Going there was our choice; we felt in control. The US offerings did not so much "reeducate" us (supposedly their purpose) – we still needed to be educated – as broaden our horizons so that the "völkisch" literature, which still surrounded us, did not shut us in.

In summertime and even in winter, my brother and I went to the Linz *Parkbad* regularly. It was built in the late twenties and early thirties and added on again and again and was already a very large complex when we were children. It had a big indoor and four different outdoor pools and lots of open spaces for sunbathing, ball playing, and picnicking. I joined both the swimming team and the diving team. On the latter, we practiced endless standing jumps so we would be able to go into the water ramrod straight and without splashing. Eventually, I advanced to a back flip and a salto forward but never became good enough to participate in any competition. In swimming, I did better. My discipline was the breaststroke, in which I made it to number two in the Austrian High School Championships. With the Swimming Club, I went to meets all over Austria, but the only thing I remember is "making out" with a boy at one of these events, i.e., necking, and afterwards, being very afraid that I might be pregnant. I was still completely uninformed about sexual matters, although my period had started when I was eleven and a half or twelve and had frightened me very much. My mother quickly calmed me down by telling me that this was normal, that it would recur, and that I was not bleeding to death as I feared. But that was the extent of her information. Despite my interest in boys, I continued to be a child. As such, I enjoyed all kinds of sports with my brother, cousins, and friends. Sometimes I taught the others, and sometimes, they taught me. In the winter, we went skiing with our father and skating by ourselves. Some of us still had skates that had to be clamped onto ordinary hiking boots. I dreamed of "real" skates and eventually got some, albeit used and brown, not white. Watching the ice dancers with admiration and envy, I taught myself the moves for dancing the waltz but had no partner. Ice-dancing was not something in which I could interest my brother or other boys I knew; they preferred hockey.

We had five busy and happy years in Linz from 1945 to 1950. Living in the center of town, we could freely go everywhere we wanted, and with our bikes, we could roam further out. Sometimes, I went for a ride on my own and collected a swarm of boys following me. It never entered my mind that this might be risky behavior. The atmosphere in which I lived was one of renewal and optimism. I did not think about it but sensed it and trusted in people and the future. I also felt that my parents were happy to be alive and with each other again. They had my aunt, her family, and my grandmother two blocks away and relatives and old friends from Vienna visiting us in the perceived safety of the US sector. People around us were happy to meet up and help each other no matter how poor their material circumstances were.

We certainly had nothing; the little furniture in our tiny apartment was all hand-me-downs; I have no idea from whom and from where. I only remember one very large and beautiful "modern" bookcase made of oak, which my family still owns. Later an awful-looking bedroom set with inlaid metal and mirrors appeared. My aunt displayed a similarly ugly dining room set when she moved into her rebuilt apartment, probably from the same source, perhaps brought on one of the covered wagons I had seen. We only had room for our ugly bedroom when we moved back to Bisamberg. I disliked this furniture intensely except for the chaiselongue, which was wonderful for reading.

Around us children still nobody talked about the past, neither about guilt nor about suffering. And I doubt that the adults among themselves did either. I was old enough now to understand a bit more and curious about conversations around me, but the snippets I overheard focused on the present and future, what practical steps family members and friends needed to take to "get back to normal," and resume their former lives, which was not possible for everybody, certainly not for my father because he had to start anew. Yet, regrets or even remembrances about the immediate past did not come up in what I gleaned from the conversations during the Saturday evening "parties."

There, the visitors from Bisamberg and Vienna reported about developments "at home." My mother's sister, Tante Mitzi, visited only once and swore she would never again cross the demarcation line between the Russian- and the American parts of Austria at Enns because the American soldiers made all passengers get off the train to spray them with DDT – against fleas and other bugs. She did not forgive them and always brought it up in later years when I saw her. My aunt did not know about the nefarious effects DDT had on the environment yet; she just resented the indignity of being sprayed and preferred the Russian soldiers who accepted their own and other people's fleas as a matter of course.

Content as we were in Linz, we could not stay. Times were indeed becoming "normal" again and changing. Our reluctant landlords wanted their full apartment back and probably had the right to reclaim it. My father received severance pay for his military service, invested it with a fruit importer, and lost it all. I once overheard my business uncles say he was too trusting and no businessman. I was quietly upset that they dared criticize my father, but they were right. He was a manager and organizer by nature and military training but had no sense for trade. He then took a job with Brown Bovery, the Swiss Electrical company, which had its main Austrian offices, not in Linz but in Vienna. My parents decided to move back to Bisamberg into my grandparents' house, to which they would build an addition. Finding affordable housing had always been difficult, especially around Vienna, and the destruction the war had wrought had not made things easier. A further consideration was my grandparents' advancing age; they needed help with their gardens and their vineyards.

Back in Bisamberg

Along with my mother, we children had already spent part of our postwar summers in Bisamberg, but the move was a major change for all of us and – at first certainly – not all positive. In Linz, everything had been within easy reach; now, the city of Vienna was far away, and public transport there was expensive. No more friends upstairs, no more cousins nearby, no more swim club, no more America House. My parents' lives became harder as well. My father probably received a reasonable salary, but it still was not lavish. Things were tight now that their earlier possessions were gone, and they had three children to raise. The building project, for which supplies were still hard to come by, took time. My father also did other chores around the house; thus, his weekends were always busy. This meant no more trips with us and fewer visits with relatives and friends. My parents still had their Saturday evenings, but for the most part, these were reduced to my Viennese aunt and uncle, Tante Mitzi, and Uncle Harry. The two of them usually spent weekends in the Bisamberg villa, where they had two rooms at first. When we were around thirteen or fourteen, we were deemed old enough to join these get-togethers but soon found them uninteresting and went our own ways.

I liked to visit the house, though, because I had fond memories of going there as a little girl. The Russians, who, like occupation forces do, had selected the biggest, most attractive house for their officers, but had already vacated it. They left their mark, albeit not the kind of destruction that they inflicted on some of the castles in the area. By the way, they did not move into the Bisamberg castle, probably because it was uninhabitable. One conspicuous sign of the short-lived occupation of my aunt's house was in its rather grand staircase, which the Russians "decorated" with large Cyrillic letters in red oil paint. It looked like verses but may also have been political slogans; nobody I knew ever bothered to find out. During the time after the War, when I went in and out, the writing was just left alone; people had other worries.

My aunt and uncle later received a third room to the two they already used. It had been the former "Herrenzimmer" [gentlemen's room] – again, there appears not to have been a salon. In part, this was a matter of naming and décor, but also of custom in the Germanophile segment of the middle and upper middle classes of Vienna that I knew of. The dining room and the dining table were the center of activity and entertainment. People, especially women, lingered around it. Only the men retired to or met in the

"Herrenzimmer" and the family joined them there. At my aunt's villa, that room was in the center of the house with a balcony onto the street. It still contained all the original furnishings, which had survived the Russians quite well. There were heavy fauteuils, a combination of bourgeois solidity with *Jugendstil* elements, in black wood and patterned plush velvet. They were not particularly comfortable or attractive – to me as a teenager who loved Scandinavian modern. The Russian officers had probably liked them, though. The only thing in that room that they had damaged was a painting, which, even in that state was, nevertheless, left hanging. It showed a famous scene from Goethe's *Faust*: Mephisto and Faust entering Auerbach's Tavern. What fascinated me was the damage. The Russians had used it for target practice. It may have been for knife throwing, but it had been, more likely, guns. Perhaps it was left hanging to hide whatever holes there were in the wall behind. Nobody talked about it. There was also a large bookcase with cut glass windows which was untouched, out of respect for German culture – I later read that some educated Russians had preserved their love for it – or, more likely, disinterest. I would have been able to guess that if I had known what the inscriptions on the staircase were, Pushkin or Stalin – or perhaps obscene remarks? The bookcase was full of heavy-looking volumes of the "German classics" and quite a few leather-bound books with Bismarck written on their spines. In contrast to my usual love of checking out bookcases, this one did not entice me.

School in Floridsdorf

My brother and I went to the R*ealgymnasium* [Austria's common university prep Junior High and High School] in Floridsdorf. It was a twenty-minute bus ride from Bisamberg. People going into Vienna then used the bus, which was more convenient and frequent than the train, and passed through the village center. There were not many cars yet. The curriculum in the Realgymnasium was and is similar all over Austria, but a small difference between the one my brother had attended in Linz and the one he would go to in

Floridsdorf made it necessary that I taught him a year's worth of English during the summer. Otherwise, he would have to repeat the first grade (the equivalent of fifth grade in the US).

In Linz, boys still started with Latin and added English in the third (eighth) grade. In Floridsdorf, boys and girls began with English – as girls had done in Linz. Our classroom was the enormous walnut tree next to my grandparents' house, where we built precarious seats in its crown. Although we normally got along very well, our lessons often ended with us in a fight and our books at the bottom of the tree. I was too impatient, and my brother too recalcitrant. Still, he passed his exam. It was my first and most challenging experience giving lessons. The following year, I started tutoring other children whose parents thought they needed help. I taught all subjects, even Math, which was not my strength, and continued giving lessons until I left university. It was a good way to earn the pocket money I needed so that I never had to ask my parents for any. I was far more patient with my other pupils than I had been with my brother, but then I was not their older sister and did not expect them to be brilliant.

My classmates in the new school welcomed me because, as one of them later told me, I was elegantly dressed – this first time. My brother had it harder; he started having fights right away, mostly on the way to or from school. His classmates eventually accepted him, but other kids did not appreciate the supercilious grin he put on when anybody attempted to bully or taunt him. He never started these fights, at least that is what I believed, but he fought back when others who were irritated by his show of contempt attacked him. He often came home with a bloody nose and torn clothes, which got him into trouble with our father. His tendency to have fights continued into young adulthood.

One later incident that I will never forget occurred in the Alps. We were a bit older and skiing in a remote area where we had to hike up to our accommodations with skis and rucksacks on our backs.

We were a group of friends, including my brother's girl, but there were other young people there as well. We danced in the evenings. The girls had one bunk room and the boys another on the floor above. Once, when we were getting ready for bed, we heard loud rumbling upstairs, and I immediately suspected that my brother had gotten into a fight; his girlfriend did too. We rushed upstairs, and sure enough, we found him lying on a bunk with a gash on his forehead. He was complaining – not about his wound, but about the fact that he had already had his drunken opponent under him but not been able to hit him in the face, a hesitation the other one clearly had not felt. I was worried and eventually convinced my brother that we had to find a doctor that very night to sow him up, or his gash would become an ugly scar. This meant skiing down to the village and finding a doctor in the middle of the night. Fortunately, another slightly older man came with us. He was quite handsome and managed to convince the female doctor, who finally opened her door, to tend to my brother. Then, the three of us trekked up the mountain again. The next day when we all left to travel back home, Klaus appeared to be all right, but in my mother's kitchen, he suddenly keeled over. Now, I had to run for our family doctor, who was considerably closer but, to my chagrin, much less concerned than the doctor in the Alps.

We were the only children from Bisamberg who went to our school, though the bus collected a few more from other villages along its route. We came to know them, but distances were such that we did not visit outside of school and were left to our own devices. We swam in the Danube and skated and played hockey on the frozen side arms. When there was snow, and there was more then, we skied on the Bisamberg. We had to hike up through the woods to a slope called "Jägerwiese" [Hunters' Meadow], which seemed steep to me then. The lords of this ski slope were young men from the local bakeries. They had finished school at fourteen and were apprentices in the many then-still-existing shops. Their days started and finished earlier than other trades. Thus, their afternoons were free –

like ours. My brother, although a bit younger than they, joined in building jumps and performing stunts. I was not interested in stunts and not good enough even if the gang had invited me into their group, which never entered their minds.

Anyway, the little slope was challenging enough for me, and at dusk, I was happy when I made it down on a steep run through the trees. I was an o.k. skier by most standards but would never become as good as both my brothers were. My younger brother cut his teeth on the same slope with a different set of bakery apprentices. Much later, when we went skiing together in the Alps – I brought my children along then – I always enjoyed watching my two brothers coming down a steep slope; their styles were so different. My younger brother appeared to glide down the most difficult terrain easily and elegantly, while the older, equally if not more skillful, always seemed to be skiing on edge. His friends called him "Tod" [death] because he chose the most difficult trails and raced in between trees.

At that time, our *Realgymnasium* in Floridsdorf was the only one in the district and the surrounding countryside. It had a girls' and a boys' section with different teachers and administrations but using the same building. Back then, mandatory school attendance ended after fourth (eighth) grade when children were fourteen. In my class, there were only ten or eleven girls who wanted to continue, too few for a separate class. Thus, it was decided to move us into the boys' school. Later, I learned that the female director of the girls' school had fought for this solution so we did not have to commute into downtown Vienna, which would have been extremely hard for me and others who came from farther away. We joined the twenty boys in our age group and became part of their school to be taught by its instructors. In Austria, they are all addressed as professors. Only our Physical Education Teacher would continue to come from the girls' school.

This coeducation, unusual for the time, was a very good experience for me and, I believe, for all of us. None of the supposed drawbacks of coeducation, such as girls keeping themselves back to not outshine the boys, held for us. They certainly did not do so for me, perhaps because I was the best student. I knew full well, though, that, girl or boy, being a good student was not what made you popular. But you were not ostracized either for being an academically bright student or a "nerd." There were no cliques and no divisions into "jocks" and "grinds," etc. We all held together well.

Much of my time and attention from fourteen on went into school and then university. I cannot say that I loved my *Realgymnasium*, only that it was a given and that I could not imagine my life without it, even if it did not occupy my days the same way High School does young people's lives in the US. Our classes were usually over by two in the early afternoon, with sports and other activities happening outside of school. Homework and studying did not take up much of my time until it came to the final examinations, the *Matura* (Abitur in Germany).

My brother and I had to help around the gardens, and I did some tutoring but still had a lot of free time. Normally, secondary school students then did not work the part-time jobs high schoolers in the US take on, whether they needed them or not. Thus, we all could pursue varied individual interests, which we chose because we liked them, not because we wanted to improve our college applications.

School brought and held us together, though, and it structured our lives. I was particularly lucky in that I never had to worry about grades; I continued to be what you call a good student, i.e., I had excellent grades. The only bad grades I ever got were in conduct, a category long since discarded from report cards. One time, I was caught reading a booklet on sex education which made the rounds. It probably was not the "right" kind, but at fourteen or fifteen, I needed anything I could lay my hands on. Another time was when

I cut class to hang out with my "demoted" boyfriend and his classmates.

Despite the occasional problems with "conduct," I was a favorite with the school's principal and with our "Klassenvorstand" [home room teacher]. The first taught us German literature and philosophy, which became one reason I love these subjects. He believed in reading and discussing and never insisted that we learn names, dates, or literary periods and movements. It was obvious to me – and my classmates – that he was fond of me, but only after I graduated did he tell me that he was in love with me. He gave me a book of German poems with an inscription in which he rephrased lines from Goethe's "Trilogie der Leidenschaft" [Trilogy of Passion], which the 72-year-old poet had written for his last great love, Ulrike von Levetzow who was 17. My principal was considerably younger than Goethe when he reworked the poem, in his fifties, but ancient as far as I was concerned. Still, not only did I enjoy his attention, but I also genuinely liked him and stayed in contact with him after graduation. He even came to my wedding. Didi, as our class called him, had the Austrian honorific title of "Hofrat" [Court Councillor], which was, and still is, awarded to civil servants of distinction, including people in education. What I did not know then and never fully understood was the rumor told me later by our Latin teacher, namely that Didi had been married to a Jewish woman but that they had divorced so his career would be protected. He never talked about this, but one time, he made a remark which stayed with me. We were discussing whether we would like to repeat the years we had already lived, and my friend Hannerl said that, yes, she would. He, however, did not want to. Much later, I heard that he had married again, a Latin "professor" at the girl's school, a very nice no-nonsense woman.

Our "Klassenvorstand," his nickname was Koscherl, taught us Latin for four years. When I look at pictures from our "Maturareise" (the class trip traditionally taken after graduation and chaperoned by the "Klassenvorstand"), I am struck by how young he looks. He was a veteran of World War II, as probably most of our instructors were, even if they did not talk about it – except for him. He could be easily distracted from Latin into war stories, which were always entertaining, never serious – while we were in school. During the first two years with him, we continued with Latin grammar, which we had started in third grade (seventh grade) of *Realgymnasium* when we were around thirteen.

I still remember our textbook, in which two Roman children travel to Vienna during the reign of Marcus Aurelius, the philosophic emperor most closely associated with our region. Some even claim he died in Vindobona, the Roman camp that became Vienna. When we moved on to reading actual texts, if you can call our painful efforts "reading," we resorted to so-called "Schmierer," unofficial translations produced for "scholars" like us and handed down from generation to generation. We needed to be careful, though, that our translations did not appear too polished. Ceasar's Latin in his *De Bello Gallico* was manageable, and I can still recite its first sentences, which came back to me when my children started looking at the French comic books of Asterix and Obelix. However, the poets, Virgil, Ovid, and Horace, were far beyond our language skills. We did not discuss them either, so they did not mean anything to us. Perhaps Koscherl made attempts to get us to appreciate what we read and was put off by our lack of interest. Still, he cannot have tried very hard. We were fond of him despite or, probably, *because* of his laissez-faire approach and kept in touch with him, with some of us doing so until his death at 106 or 107.

As long as he possibly could, he joined our yearly class reunions, for which the organizers picked places close to his home. His 100th birthday was quite a party, I heard. Since these reunions were held in late spring, I could not attend them while I was still teaching in the US. One time though, when I was in Vienna on a sabbatical and walked into the get-together hesitantly, not knowing if I would recognize anybody, he was the first to greet me. He had even read my books on Anna Seghers, whose life and works as a Communist

142

were totally beyond his conservative Catholic interests. He knew that I would be there and brought the books with him so I could sign them. I was more touched than flattered.

Thereafter, no matter when I came to Vienna, he invited me to his lovely old villa, where he lived by himself into his nineties. With advancing age, he lost his previous discretion and told stories that became ever darker and less coherent. He was plagued by war memories and a sense of guilt, although he had served as a radio operator and claimed he never killed anybody. The one time he had been ordered to shoot hostages, he went to a church to pray and then refused, fully expecting to be shot himself. However, a counterattack spared him. It was a story he told others as well, so I did not doubt its veracity but wondered about the change in tone of his war tales from our school days. Another story he told me – and probably others – had to do with his wife. She was a young mother and was raped by Russian soldiers. After that, she never let him touch her, which must have made the marriage very difficult – for her and for him. When we were his pupils, we had no idea about all of this, but then there must have been many stories of suffering and guilt hidden in our teachers and other adults around us. They smoldered under a thin surface which they kept intact as long as they could and which we did not know how to break, nor did we want to.

Among Koscherl's late confessions was also the crush that he supposedly had on me during our common school days. When I visited him in his old age, he made much of this infatuation, which became embarrassing to me, especially if his son was around. Perhaps he just vented the phantasies of an old man who was alone most of the time. The home in which he spent his last years was a Catholic institution, expensive and good, as such places go. The staff treated the "Herr Professor" respectfully and kindly, but they all came from Eastern Europe and had limited German. By then, he had few visitors and little chance to talk. When I visited this home, rarely enough, and with a classmate who attended to him much

143

more regularly, his ramblings became ever more obsessed with war and guilt without ever referring to a specific incident. My friend, a faithful Catholic like him and a genuinely good person, was no-nonsense and ignored these ramblings. But to me, the visits became increasingly painful. Having lost my parents early, Koscherl was my only exposure to very old age in a generation that had gone through World War II and its aftermath and was full of secrets and suppressed guilt. While he had been lucid, his Catholic faith had supported Koscherl, but when his mind and memory failed him, his faith did as well. It appeared to only increase his confusion and pain.

We had other memorable "professors" as teachers at our school. Joule – this was the nickname we gave him – taught physics and chemistry. Rumors circulated that he had been a university professor who was "demoted" to secondary school teaching because of his Nazi affiliation. Nobody talked openly about it, though. Besides, there were so many other former Nazis in our school who could not be demoted further; they were needed and just stayed. Teachers, especially male ones, were in short supply. Joule was an ungainly man with a big bald head who appeared kindly to me. Although I was not really interested in his subjects, I had good grades there as well – most of the time.

As was the custom in all classes without written tests, instructors called students up individually and examined them in front of the class. Usually, they did so only at grading time, and we could prepare. One time, though, Joule examined me when I did not expect it, and I failed miserably. He allowed me to make up my bad grade but must have had a low opinion of me and probably all females in the sciences, which he displayed in our tiny chemistry lab when he took a precious test tube out of my clumsy hands and said, "Leave that alone, you'll get your 1 [A] anyway."

Still, when we came close to the "Matura," I chose chemistry as my science subject for the oral. Joule gave me his questions ahead of time, which was very much against the rules. To the surprise of the examining school inspector and the whole committee before which we had to appear, I was stupid enough to rattle off the periodic tables which I had learned by heart. I do not remember how Joule saved the situation – and himself. At the time, I thought of him as just being good to me. Now, I wonder if his behavior, besides showing a lack of respect for girls in the sciences, did not express his contempt for the whole postwar situation and system. He knew, what I would only understand much later, that many who were in power in Austria after the war, including those in the educational establishment, were also fascists, but so-called Austro-Fascists, who had ruled the country since their victory over the Social Democrats in 1934. When the Nazis took over four years later, they persecuted those fascists along with all others who did not support them, such as socialists or communists. After the war, the Austro-Fascist, some of whom had been interred in concentration camps, were vindicated and on top. Besides them, there were enough old Nazis who had buried their past more successfully than Joule had.

The only "professor" I thoroughly disliked taught geography and history, of course, never contemporary history. We knew nothing about him except that he was a strict authoritarian. He pranced around in jackboots, swishing what looked like a riding crop against them. It was his pointer, but this man fit the image of fascists as movies later depicted them, except that, at the time, I had not seen one yet. I just hated the man and his behavior. Everybody else showed great respect towards him, even my brothers, whom he also taught. I detested him because of the sadistic streak that, to me, appeared to be particularly strong in him. He seemed to relish students' failures and made it extremely hard to help those who were called in front of the class to be examined. I sat in the first row and tried to pass on answers but failed with him, perhaps an additional reason I detested him.

In general, though, we liked our teachers, even if there was a kind of almost sporty "us versus them" ambiance. Cheating was something everybody took part in when they needed to, and good or well-prepared students helped others; that was an unspoken obligation. Personally, I thought many teachers, not just the one who intimidated us with his boots and "switch," had a sadistic streak. Examinations, I felt, were designed to ferret out what we did not know. Instructors quickly singled out the weaker students and called on them more frequently and out of the blue. I always considered this most unfair. One person who behaved egregiously in this respect was our only female "professor." She was a very competent English teacher with whom we learned a lot. However, the boys did not respect her as they did the strict and demanding male teachers and, instead, called her a witch.

Classmates

One young man in particular whose lack of preparedness and – she implied – intelligence drew her ire the minute she entered the class. What may have set her against him, even more, was the fact that he did not care. He was from a prosperous Floridsdorf family which dealt in building materials, for many years a very sought-after commodity, and had a big mouth. But all he wanted to do was enjoy himself, get through school, and finish with the *Matura*, which he did. Most of my male classmates went on to university and became highly respected professionals, he is one of the few who did not, but he fared very well anyway. When I see him now, he is still the life of the party. He went on to marry an intelligent and competent woman, has children and grandchildren, and even boasts about the many concerts and plays he attends. The English teacher left no scars, and his classmates liked him then and still do.

The girls in our class were a mixed group and held together despite our differences; there were so few of us. Uli, my closest friend in fifth and sixth grade, left school early to get married. Then, my best friend who sat next to me in the first row was Hannerl, the most attractive girl in our class. After graduation, she started studying business, but I lost her as well because she contracted tuberculosis and left Austria for a warmer climate, where she married her doctor.

146

When she contacted me once many years later after her husband had died, she seemed dissatisfied with her life. Then, she disappeared again. Another classmate, to whom I never became close, was the perfect "lady" then and remained one into old age, always concerned with appearances, elegantly dressed, and well made up at fifteen as well as at eighty. There was also Maria, who sat next to her but was the very opposite. Down-to-earth then, she became even more so as she grew older. She was a painter and an environmentalist who lived in an old mill in the north of Austria. Married to and separated from another painter who gave her several children but no support, prioritizing his own career, she is the only one in our class who now struggles financially. She was and still is a warm, lovely person. We had another Hannerl – short for Johanna, a very popular name in Austria – whom all the boys liked very much. Although she was not particularly pretty, she was pleasant and domestic. She must have retained her appeal because, after a failed marriage, she ended up with a much younger man.

With Hannerl

 Only one of my female classmates finished university, Erika, a sporty woman who became a "professor" of Physical Education and another subject I do not recall. She eventually married the most attractive young man in our class. When she died of cancer after they had spent a long and happy life together, he was devastated.

In academic terms, Liese was the most interesting. She went into medical technology, worked in a laboratory, and, after her retirement, studied history to keep her brain active. She received a master's degree and published a book on medical doctors at the University of Vienna during the Middle Ages. It was published, and she was honored, when the university celebrated its 650th anniversary in 2010. After that, she continued working on medieval documents in the period's difficult Latin until her death in 1922. Liese never married but had a Klosterneuburg canon as a boyfriend. I also vaguely remember two large girls who, as best I recall, were never ill-treated, or made fun of, yet were a bit on the margin. Many years later, one of them contacted me in the US and wanted to visit, but I did not recognize her name and responded evasively. She had not left an impression on me. When I found out who she was, I was sorry. Now, I wonder how she and the other girl felt during our shared time in school, although they do attend class reunions, which suggests they have good memories.

The more I think about my classmates in the Floridsdorf *Realgymnasium,* the more stories come to mind. One of the boys became an acknowledged and successful contemporary composer. Some of the others not only attend his concerts but are regular concertgoers in general. They are very knowledgeable about music and play a variety of instruments. Yet, during our school days, none of them talked about these interests and skills. When, a few years ago, I expressed my surprise at that, I was told, "Of course not; you could not attract girls with this kind of talk." I was taken aback, but it is true. Artistic and intellectual interests were played down rather than up. It was okay to discuss such things during class but not outside class.

However, as I mentioned, school did not fill our days completely. We all had room for a variety of "extracurricular" activities. Sports, except for unpopular gym classes, happened outside and independently in sports clubs. A classmate even played as a goalie for one of Vienna's big soccer clubs, which gained him a great deal of respect not only with the others but with our teachers as well, even if he was not the brightest of students. He was among the third of boys who had to take Russian as their first foreign language, while the rest could start with English. Our school was in the Russian sector. The modest language skills my classmate, Toberl, acquired, combined with his sports activities and connections,

149

served him very well after graduation: he conducted business beyond the Iron Curtain and earned a lot of money, not all totally above board, as he hinted in a later conversation with me.

Graduation from the *Realgymnasium* or *Gymnasium* involves a set of oral and written examinations watched over by outside inspectors from the Ministry of Education. This final set of examinations is called *Matura* in Austria and *Abitur* in Germany. Then it was all you needed to be allowed to attend university. Much later, the "numerus clausus" was introduced, which for many highly sought subjects demands that you have an excellent grade average and fulfill other requirements as well because there are too many applicants. For us, this was not yet a problem. I studied more for the Matura than I had ever done before. Often, I did what I still like to do, wrap myself in a blanket and lie in a deckchair in the garden. Sometimes, I got up to check if the bulbs I had planted in the fall were finally sprouting. They took their time, but there were many other signs of early spring which I enjoyed observing. My lifelong love of gardening probably received a boost more than my love of chemistry which I ostensibly studied. At the written exams, we were seated far apart and carefully monitored, yet I remember passing my answers to the math problems to a classmate behind me for copying. He was so anxious that he did not get them back to me for a while, and I trembled that we would both be caught, which would have meant no *Matura* and no university. Ironically, I was not that good at math myself, and, for many years, I dreamt that I could not answer the math questions at the Matura. Yet there was this unspoken rule that you had to respond to appeals for help. At least, that is what I felt. Anyway, we all passed, and I and one or two others did so with distinction.

One customary reward was/is the "Maturareise," a trip the whole class takes together. In comparison to today, this was a big deal then, none of us was that well-traveled. Thus, the purpose of this extended outing was twofold, to expand our horizons and spend time with our classmates one last time – without any school obligations. We had to raise some money to help the few people for whom the modest expense was still too much. I was chosen to participate in Austria's most popular radio quiz program – we did not have TVs yet – which gave monetary and other prizes. This could have ended in a disaster because I discovered then and there that I was not quick enough on my feet at such events. However, the kindly and beloved quizmaster, who knew about the purpose of my participation, helped me win after all. I did not tell anybody that we had cheated, gave the money to our group, and used the other prizes as I saw fit: a ship excursion on the Danube to my younger brother and a restaurant meal for two, to which I invited my grandfather.

The class chose northern Italy, the Lago di Garda, where we slept in tents on a campground right by the lake. It was wonderful to sunbathe on the rocks that jotted out from the water while chatting and laughing. We were all crazy about getting the perfect suntan, not knowing yet about the dangers of over-exposure to the sun. However, we did worry about the supposedly poisonous snakes which we sometimes spotted swimming around. I am very afraid of snakes, poisonous or not. From our camp, we made day trips to Verona, Florence, and Venice.

Our "Maturareise" was lovely and fun, but I had one big disappointment: Venice. St. Mark's cathedral struck me as dusty and the town as dirty, not the luminous city of poetry I had expected. Unfortunately, this disappointment prevented me from ever going back. At first, my memories and later the reports about crowds of tourists choking the place kept me away. Perhaps I will try again. Perhaps Venice, the beautiful, will never materialize for me.

In Verona, we attended an opera in the town's outdoor arena; I believe we saw *Aida*. It was the ambiance that left a profound impression on me, though, because it was a feast and a spectacle that was quite different from what I had become accustomed to from Vienna. People came with food, drink, and even portable radios and applauded every aria they liked, which was then repeated, all absolute tabus at the Vienna State Opera. We were at the arena in Verona long past midnight, but the singers did not appear to mind.

Florence found me unprepared. I knew little about art then and almost nothing about the Renaissance. We had had art education in school, which meant producing collages of flowerpots, drawing, and painting, skills in which I had no talent and little interest. Often our teacher let me read to the class while they pursued their projects, and he drew me. How he decided on my grade, which was good enough, I do not know. While I never learned to draw or paint – I doubt the others who were not already talented did either. I later became very interested in art and art history and now wonder why our teacher never thought of taking us to visit at least one of Vienna's great Art Museums. We always went on hikes or week-long skiing trips.

Another graduation ritual was a party with our instructors. It was different from the annual ball our school held, more informal and just for our class. What I do recall about it is embarrassing. But, most of it, I cannot remember at all, which is even more embarrassing. Sitting at a table with the school's principal and I do not know who else, I paid no attention to how much I drank – too much, as it turned out. Without the slightest warning, I passed out, not physically, "only" mentally. From that moment on, I had no recollection whatsoever of my actions, only to be told afterwards by two classmates that I had continued dancing with the principal in a very suggestive way and had shocked everybody. How I got home, I do not know. The next day I had a terrible hangover which my father commented by saying, "Good, you will remember."

I did not remember, though, and had the same thing happen to me once more at a New Year's Eve party. Again, I had no recollection of what I had done. From then on, I was careful. I knew I could drink quite a bit without becoming tipsy or slurring my speech to warn me. Of course, I could have decided to never drink anything at all, but that was not the culture I grew up with. Besides, I loved wine. It was the only alcoholic drink I really liked.

Boyfriends

By the age of fourteen, I was very interested in boys and continued to be drawn to the ones with a "bad reputation." One of my new classmates, Herbert, was older than the rest – he had already repeated a class – and became my special friend. He wore a leather jacket, smoked, and could not care less about school. His hero was Marlon Brando, but he also talked about joining the French Foreign Legion. In class, he sat on the other side of a small gangway from me, where I tried to help him during tests by passing answers across. But it was to no avail; he had to repeat that class as well.

I continued to spend time with him, though, often in school, where a few of his new classmates joined us in hanging out in an empty hallway or room. We all cut our classes. I remember this because, over the years, I kept hearing and reading about one of those kids who eventually became the Finance Minister of Austria and had a good chance of making it to chancellor but got involved in more corruption than was acceptable under his mentor, Austria's one great chancellor, Bruno Kreisky. No worry, he did very well for himself, becoming director of Austria's major bank. To my recent surprise, he also edited a very good book on the history of the Social Democratic Party in Austria. Of course, he had quite a lot of help, but it was, nevertheless, a substantial achievement. I do not know what happened to my friend, but I heard vaguely that he, too, fared rather well, perhaps because of his connections which were/are important in Austria.

For a year or two, in our fifth and perhaps sixth grade, Herbert was also my escort to the theater. Vienna had, and I believe still has, this wonderful institution called "Theater der Jugend" [Young People's Theater], which allowed us to buy cheap tickets. My girlfriend Uli and I went frequently. She was with another boy from our class. I do not recall discussing the plays afterwards, but I do remember going to Vienna's big *Stadtpark* [City Park]. It has the river Wien flowing through it, which in normal times is no more than a trickle but caused major devastation during floods. When the Ringstraße was being built, the *Stadtpark* was to run along part of it and to safely contain the Wien. For that purpose, the river was encased in high concrete walls with architecturally elaborate staircases leading down from the level of the park to the "natural" river bed. There was a walkway down there with benches along the walls and lights high above, which left things quite dim. That is where we went after the theater to cuddle and kiss. One time, a policeman came through and scared us away, telling us we were much too young and had no business being there. I do not know if these sparsely lit areas were unsafe then. Now, I would hesitate to go there at night, but then we did not even think of being afraid and probably had no reason to be.

At that time, the ensembles of the Burgtheater and of the Vienna Opera, which we mostly attended, performed nearby in the lovely and intimate "Theater an der Wien" [Theater on the Wien], which is associated with Mozart, and in the Ronacher," another of the many venues for theatrical and musical performances Vienna's spectacle hungry population had enjoyed for many years. Their own houses which had received pride of place on the Ringstraße, had been destroyed at the end of the war and were being rebuilt according to the original plans, which was a priority for the country and took until 1955 when the Burgtheater was reopened with Grillparzer's "König Ottokars Glück und Ende" [King Ottokar's Good Fortune and End]. The play is a celebration of the founding of Austria under the Habsburgs. I saw it, of course, albeit not on opening night. The Vienna State Opera performed Beethoven's Fidelio.

Throughout my school and university years, I attended the Burgtheater faithfully, more faithfully even than the Opera, wanting to take in every new production. It was, and is, considered the preeminent German-language stage, but at the time and frequently throughout its existence, it was very conservative, playing mostly "classics" and safe, well-established authors. Great acting was very important, and I, along with many others, admired several actors who had already had thriving careers under the Nazis. Their past was not talked about. Besides, nobody cared. Being a standing member of the ensemble was a civil service position and not easily lost. As already mentioned, some of the actors, whose names I still remember, had also been in infamous Nazi films and continued their movie and theater careers after the war. While I quickly forget contemporary actors, the names of the men and women I saw then have stayed with me. The Hörbiger brothers – Attila was married to Paula Wessely – even started an acting dynasty, with the daughters and granddaughters later also performing in the *Burgtheater*, on TV, and in films.

When I was fourteen or fifteen, I had some local boyfriends as well. Two were distant cousins. One was attractive and pleasant but not very interesting. The other, less attractive and less secure, came one time to pick me up only to introduce me to some friends who had motorcycles and took me for a ride and a visit to an inn without inviting him along. I should have objected but did not understand what was going on right away, that he was acting as a kind of panderer. They behaved well toward me. Still, I did not see them again and lost my respect for him. However, he had impressed me earlier by inviting me to my first film in downtown Vienna, *Gone with the Wind*. It played only in one movie house in the original language and was wonderful and quite different from the usual fare in our neighborhood cinema. To make it in time, we even took a cab, then a very unusual experience for me. I do not know what became of him. Of the other one, I heard much later that he had turned into a regular at the local "Heurigen" and somewhat of a lush. His mother was a cousin of my mother's, so I heard about him when I visited. I never saw him again, though.

Confirmation and Balls

Confirmation for Lutherans is at fourteen and a big event, preceded by regular lessons and culminating in an examination and a ceremony in the church, an appropriate confirmation dress, and a family party afterwards. Besides the lessons for confirmation, I was active in the Lutheran church and participated in its youth group for girls, which I enjoyed very much. The minister's wife made us feel comfortable and treated us as young adults. Together, we read and discussed books about the history of Lutherans in Austria, which made them interesting to me because they were presented as intrepid outsiders. I also had my own circle of smaller children with whom I met once a week for fun and games, but I was at a loss when I thought I had to teach them about religion. I knew the Bible stories but was no longer sure about my own faith and did not want to be a hypocrite. Honesty about faith meant a lot to me, perhaps because there was so much dishonesty and lip service in the Catholic church around me.

Lutherans, I thought, were more upright. However, one of the girls in my circle and in the confirmation class, whom I admired because she was particularly pious, gave me a lesson in hypocrisy and accommodation on the part of a Lutheran. She was the only daughter of the owner of the biggest patisserie in the neighboring town. Not only did she go on to marry a Catholic pastry chef, an important and well-regulated profession in Austria, but to convert to Catholicism herself. As she explained it to me, business considerations pushed aside her supposedly strong Lutheran faith. This disappointed me, who had worried about being a much less firm believer. I never went to her bakery again, although I knew full well that – probably in part due to the husband – it became the best in the area. Her father had died in the war, and her mother had held the business together, but the two women were an example of the postwar situation, which I did not understand at the time. Despite the many competent women who carried on singlehandedly during and after the War, a large number still felt they needed a man, whatever the price.

If confirmation was one important step towards adulthood for a Lutheran girl, attendance at balls a few years later was another – for all young middle and upper-class women. As was and still is the custom, my girlfriend Uli and I attended dancing lessons around the age of sixteen. We went to the local dancing school organized by a fraternity that was big in our *Realgymnasium*. The most famous dancing school in downtown Vienna, Ellmayer, was too far to get to every week. When we "graduated" from our lessons, we received our first gowns and were deemed ready to attend balls and attract suitors. This was the pattern in the 19th century and the one my girlfriend Uli, who had seemed such a free spirit, followed. Her father, a lawyer, took her to some of the big balls in Vienna, first and foremost that of his professional organization – every organization has its own ball, the most prestigious being that of the Vienna Philharmonic Orchestra.

At this point, my and my girlfriend's paths separated. She met a man, probably also a lawyer, who worked for Austrian radio and was apparently considered an appropriate suitor by her parents. Things moved quickly then. I saw her, for the last time, I believe, when she stopped by my house – her suitor had a motorcycle – to tell me that they had made love on the Bisamberg and that it had been wonderful. She then left school, got married at sixteen, and disappeared into the adult world. I do not think she was pregnant, but I do not know. We had shared everything, and suddenly, all communication stopped. I was not even invited to her wedding and never heard from her again. Perhaps she got caught up in all the preparations for her new life. As I think about things now, it all appears strange, but, at the time, I took what happened for granted and did not give it much thought. I only missed her and knew that what she did was not what I wanted. Now, I cannot help but wonder how her life, which started along 19th-century lines, turned out in the second half of the 20th. When I later asked our former classmates about Uli, none of them knew anything.

With Herbert (on the left), Uli (on the right, leaning back) and Other Classmates

I received a lovely ballgown as well, which my mother made for me and redesigned a few times, but at first, I only attended smaller events to which my mother had to take me since my father did not want to. He only came along once or twice when my brother was old enough to join us and brought his girlfriend. My father's refusal was hurtful, especially since he did not give a reason. Now, I understand that he probably wanted to play a more prominent role than he could with only my mother and me and not knowing others. Soon, I was no longer dependent on family; friends invited me to some of the big balls in Vienna, which I enjoyed greatly. I was not looking for a husband my parents approved but for fun.

Fredy

Another of my friends in the Lutheran girls' group had a much older brother whom she introduced to me at a fair in the neighboring village. Everybody called him Fredy, which now sounds funny to me. He squired me around at the fair, shot some paper roses for me, and soon became my first serious boyfriend. I was not yet sixteen when I met him; he was twelve years my senior. At first, I was flattered by his attention. He was attractive and an excellent dancer. All the girls and women envied me. There were not many young men his age around. His circle of friends, with whom I started to spend time as well, were students at the university. They were older than I but younger than him.

None of them had been a soldier; *he* had. Indeed, he had been in the *Waffen SS*, division "Totenkopf" [skull]. He made no secret of it, on the contrary. However, he claimed that he had been in a tank unit fighting on the front which was not to be confused with the "other SS." And he proudly displayed his photograph in the black uniform, which I considered quite handsome. I knew nothing about the SS nor his distinctions, although this now strikes me as hard to believe. Nobody held his past against him. In fact, nobody asked about it. He himself stressed his Arian descent, with his father or his father's family having originally come from Persia.

In the beginning, he was not the only one from his group interested in me. There was also a younger friend, a student of journalism. I had noticed "Kater" [tomcat], as he was called, on the bus we all used to go downtown and had liked the way he looked. After a dance, he walked me and my grandmother, who had attended as a chaperone, home and asked for a date. We met by the Danube and just talked. Then, I did not hear from him again. Fredy finally told me that the two of them had discussed me and that Kater had agreed to step back, saying that he would have to work too hard to educate me so I would become the way he wanted me! Supposedly, he also bragged that we had sex together, even though we had not even kissed. Indeed, Kater had been gentle and respectful, and I liked him for that. However, I believe the kind of talk and bargaining that went on behind my back, as if I were a piece of property, was not that unusual among men in Austria at the time. Still, it offended me very much when I heard about it.

All this ended up throwing me back onto Fredy, who professed his "eternal love" and swore he could not live without me. I had no idea if what he told me about Kater was true and had no way of checking. None of us had a phone, and we lived too far apart. Kater would have had to make a special effort to stay in touch with me, which he did not do. As for me, the thought of letting him know I liked him never even entered my mind. I expected to be wooed. Thus, I did not see him again; he even withdrew from his friends. Fredy had beaten him. Unfortunately for Fredy, I was not the prize he thought me to be because it turned out that I was not that fond of him, not to speak of being in love, about which I knew nothing. I did not even respect him, just took him for granted. What helped Fredy was that my parents did not approve of him and that he was persistent. Looking back, I realize that I was quite naïve and selfish in our relationship. For a few years, he served as a distinguished-looking escort who took me to dances and the theater when I wanted. On weekends, we spent time with his friends, who belonged to the establishment of the neighboring town and were good company.

Naturally, Fredy seduced me – if you can call it that. Having been a soldier, a US prisoner of war, and then having worked for the US military, he had more experience and knowledge in sexual matters than all the young men around him who looked up to him. I, of course, still knew nothing but was curious and let him fondle me until, at one point, he said, "'It' has already happened by mistake, and now, you might as well let me make real love to you."

I allowed this, perhaps because I believed him and expected more – excitement, pleasure – which never came. Perhaps I was too young; perhaps all his experience had been more quantity than quality.

From then on, Fredy kept begging, and I sometimes relented but was never really interested. The fondest memory I have of being alone with him is a daylong kayak trip up the sidearms of the Danube. It was a weekday, for which I had cut class, and he had taken a day off from work, and it was spring. The only human we saw all day, besides the waiter at an inn on the Danube where we had lunch, was a lonely Russian soldier trying to fish. I had my period, so he accepted that I would not allow any sex. Then, I was happy in his company and in the nature around us, which he also appreciated and knew well. It was still early in our relationship, and the most beautiful day I ever had with him.

I spent five years with Fredy. Why did I not break up with a man I did not love or even respect? There was this comfortable selfishness on my part, and there were his constant protestations that he could not live without me. During my last years of school and my first years at university, he was always available. He was somebody with whom I could spend my free time and do things I enjoyed. I was not really attracted to anybody else, although I did see other young men occasionally, and for a while, there was a fellow student I met up with in Vienna. He had a car and access to an apartment in the city. We shared things in common during the week, went on outings, read poetry, and frequented the Diana Bad. He studied English and Physical Education, was attractive, and felt very proud of his body, but we never slept with each other. Our friendship ended when one of his many aunts, who owned a house in Bisamberg, told him that I already had a boyfriend. He immediately broke off our relationship, perhaps out of wounded pride, although I never thought that what we had was more than a friendship. Still, I liked his company and was sorry to lose it.

Eventually, shortly after my twenty-first birthday, Fredy decided that he could indeed live without me – and quite well. Out of the blue, he told me that the daughter of his boss was expecting a baby from him and that he had to marry her. It was a serious blow, mostly to my vanity but also to my trust and self-confidence. However, even then, I thought that the separation was a good thing and that his shabby behavior served me right because I had been too selfish, passive, and also loyal to leave him of my own accord.

When he tried to get together again – how seriously, I do not know – my pride recovered a bit. Still, his very public desertion was painful, even if it turned out to be the best thing that could have happened to me. I would have been miserable with him, and he, with me. I shudder to think about the life we would have had. Fredy's story about the baby may have been an elaborate hoax to get out of our relationship, but he did have a child and did get married to the original woman's sister, it appears. It is all quite murky. I refused to ask anybody about him, so I only knew what people told me. More than fifty years later, I met his much younger half-brother on a rowing trip and heard from that man's wife, who had no idea who I was, that Fredy had died. He had fathered many more children, the last one when he was in his seventies. This must have been with another, even younger woman.

With Fredy

My times with Fredy were not all bad, though; quite to the contrary, I just always thought I should be in love, which I knew I was not, even if I did not really know how that felt. He was attractive and attentive, and genuinely liked dancing, especially to jazz and swing music. When Harry James came to Vienna with his band, we had to be there. We also went to the city's one major jazz cellar, with a trumpeter called Fatty George as its star attraction and Friedrich Gulda, a famous classical pianist, sometimes at the piano. In our last year together, we took extra dancing lessons so we could learn new steps and moves to the tango, samba, rumba, and czardas. I was a poorer dancer than him, but as a couple, we sometimes had people stop to watch us, even when we just waltzed. I never again had a partner with whom the most elaborate dance appeared so effortless.

Waltzing with Fredy

Alemannia

Fredy also did something – for my brother and me – which lasted long beyond his presence in my life: He introduced both of us to his rowing club in Korneuburg. He, himself, was only interested in kayaking and just stored his Klepper kayak in the rowing club's boathouse. But my brother and I got seriously into rowing, my brother more deeply than I. The club had been founded in 1905, and some of the original competitive rowers were still active as chairmen and board members. Its Teutonic name, Alemannia, reflected the atmosphere around the club's inception, inspired by the then-popular German author I previously mentioned, Felix Dahn. Even our rowboats had arcane Germanic names, such as Widigab or Adalgar, after Dahn's heroes.

Like ships and yachts, our boats were christened in a ceremony. They needed a name, not only because of custom, but because whenever you took a boat out on the water, you had to record this fact in a big logbook in the boathouse: time, destination, rowers, and return – well-cleaned. We had to put the boats on special sawhorses to hose and wipe them down before we put them back. When my brother and I joined, the club was heading towards a high point. It owned quite a few boats, sleek ones for racing and sturdier ones for excursions, and it had many young members that were my brother's age.

Although I did participate actively, especially in training and competitions, I was a bit of an outsider at first because of my association with Fredy and, later, because I was a little older than the others. Still, the girls in my boat became good friends.

The boathouse and adjoining fenced-in lawn were at a point along the Danube where a sidearm split off. This sidearm led to a shipyard that was in Russian hands. Thus, we did not go farther into it, but we had a dock at its beginning where there was no current, and launching a boat was easy. Then, however, you had to steer around a promontory and into the Danube, a tricky maneuver because we always rowed upriver. The current was strong, so we had to stay close to the embankment, which, on our side, consisted of the large boulders I already mentioned. Steering, which I often did, was a challenge, especially in the more fragile racing boats, which were quite costly. We, the younger people, knew that and tried to be good stewards but left the finances to the older, established club members, who were successful businessmen and civil servants from Korneuburg and Vienna. Rowing was not a proletarian sport, something I never thought about.

On summer weekends, boats, including an eight-seater, often rowed up to Muckendorf, a village near the town of Tulln, whose name [Mücke = Mosquito] accurately spoke of the swarms of mosquitoes that plagued you most ferociously in the sidearms and woods along the Danube. They were somewhat less evil on the river itself. At any rate, you had to suffer while rowing; you could not just drop your oars and swat at a mosquito. Supposedly after a while, you developed immunity, but I never did. Muckendorf, however, was a popular destination because it was at a challenging but manageable distance and had a very good inn on an inlet where we could "park" the boats and have a late Sunday lunch. The inn served enormous *Schnitzel,* which the young men who provided the muscle for the older club members were customarily treated to. On these excursions, the boats usually carried a mix of generations but not of gender. The girls rowed separate boats; they did not provide enough muscle for others but could pull their own weight and did buy their own Schnitzel. The older women did not want to go on such strenuous trips; they preferred to stay in the boathouse and socialize there.

Going back home downriver in the afternoon was easy. We steered into the middle of the Danube and let its current float us down. We even stretched out as best we could but had to keep an eye out for passing ships to avoid collisions and deal with the waves we loved so much when swimming. Now they were a problem. We had to sit

167

up quickly, steer the boat into the right position vis-à-vis the waves, adjust the oars and let them glide in orderly formation or even row carefully. If we did not manage all that properly, our boat took on water and went under, which was a minor disaster. In such a case, we had to hold on to the boat, swim it to where it could be beached, take the long cumbersome oars off, empty the boat, and fit the oars in again. Then, all drenched, we could clamber in to continue our journey. Thank goodness, on the other side of the Danube from us, there were gravel banks which made all that easier, and fortunately, such accidents did not happen often and were not dangerous – we thought. Somehow, we felt at home on the river.

Besides participating in longer or shorter trips, sometimes with overnights in tents or as guests at another rowing club up the Danube, we competed in races. My brother and his partner did so in a two-seater boat, a sweep or a double skull. They also competed in a four and, less frequently, an eight. Wolfgang, the partner, was huge and seemed clumsy intellectually and physically, but he later led the most adventurous life of us all, moving to Australia, first to hunt crocodiles, then to build his own catamaran and sail around the world. In terms of rowing "success," the girls' coxed four did best.

Our Boat Training

We became Austrian champions – against very little competition – and were sent to European championships, one in Macon, France, and one near London. The Olympic Games did not allow women rowers at the time, not that we would have had a chance. In the international meets, we always lost against the Eastern Europeans, who greatly outmatched us, physically and in terms of speed. We gave our best, but mostly we had fun. While the Eastern Europeans were watched over by their trainers and functionaries and could not attend dances, we could, and we did, although we had our share of old-men-functionaries who came along and tried to wield their influence – to little avail. Unfortunately, at one point – I do not recall when or where – all our bathing suits, which we had hung over our dressing room doors to dry, were gone. We suspected East Europeans but did not make a fuss. I wondered, though, if any of those big athletic women could fit into my suit. At the time, Austria took pride in two male Olympic rowers, silver medalists, who came along to the European championships. I liked them and saw them a few times outside of competitions. They were more assiduous about training than we ever were, although nobody took it so seriously

169

that it diminished enjoyment of the sport – at least, that was my perception.

The Boat at the European Championships: Hemma, Rosi, Ingrid, Me

At the Alemannia, boys, and girls had the same trainer, not a professional and perhaps not even an oarsman. Herr Mach, as we called him, was a one-legged former SA man who was willing and, thus, charged to work with us young people. I do not know if he was paid by the club, but he was certainly looked down upon by the club's establishment as if he were a hired hand. We, his charges, did not care, we respected him well enough for training purposes, and otherwise, he let everybody be and did not assert his authority. He did not interfere in the occasional tensions between the young people and their elders, who often were the parents. Parties and music were too loud, and messes were not cleaned up properly, etc. By the way, the fact that Herr Mach had a leg prosthesis, which he snapped off and on, was not so unusual at the time. The club's president and later president of the Austrian Rowing Federation also left his prosthesis on the dock when he heaved himself into a boat to row, which he still did regularly. As a former aristocrat – in Austria, you were no longer allowed to use the "von" indicating nobility – whose family had lived in Korneuburg, he was one of the club's early competitive rowers and an army officer during World War II. When Austria built up its own army again in the late fifties, he joined and became one of its generals.

Ingrid, his daughter, was my brother's age and his first girlfriend. Attractive, fun-loving, a good sportswoman, and a born leader, she also was the stroke oar of our boat. Like all the young people in the club, she loved to dance. On weekends and when it was too cold for rowing, we had parties and even a big ball in Korneuburg, which some of us opened with a Polonaise. We had to practice for it but were rewarded by the waltz, which it ended on, and where we had the usually crowded dance floor to ourselves.

Fredy and I participated in the dances and the balls, with him serving as something of a teacher to the younger kids. His best friend's band, for which he acted as a kind of manager, played at this and other events. My brother – I do not remember if he ever took dancing lessons, but he probably did like everybody else – also became an excellent dancer, especially of the popular boogie-woogie with all its acrobatics. I am pretty sure his girlfriend attended Ellmayer, where you had to wear white gloves and were taught good manners along with the traditional dances, never boogie-woogie. She enjoyed the activities at the rowing club more, though. Still, my brother grew tired of her, or really, of the demands her mother made. He had to bring Ingrid home after every event they attended, a reasonable request under normal circumstances, only Ingrid lived in downtown Vienna, and he had to walk home on foot in the middle of the night, which took an hour and a half or more. A taxi was out of the question then. My brother never complained, and I doubt that this inconvenience was the major reason that he turned his attention to another girl in our boat. He probably just liked her easy-going ways more and found Ingrid high maintenance. He never talked about it, but Ingrid confessed her disappointment to me. Still, she was a good sport and remained friends with my brother and her "rival." I felt sorry for her and admired her fortitude, particularly when I found out that her mother, whom we all perceived as snobby and difficult, was very ill with cancer. She eventually died, with her only daughter taking care of her throughout. Much later, Ingrid married an officer in the Austrian army. I happened to be in Vienna then and attended her wedding in the grand Charles Church with the rest of our long-since-disbanded boat crew. I do not know what happened to her later, but I vaguely heard that she died young.

Unfortunately, Anneliese, her successor with my brother, died even younger. She was an attractive happy-go-lucky girl who lived in the next village. Like the rest of us, she went everywhere on her bike using Bundesstraße 1, which connected our village to Vienna in one direction and Korneuburg in the other. Over the years, it became busier and busier with cars and trucks. In 1962, Anneliese was on her way to my brother to bring him papers for a motorcycle he had just bought when she was hit by a drunk driver and instantly killed. By then, I was married and living in Paris. Worried about my brother, who was devastated by the loss and his feelings of guilt that she had been killed while doing something for him, I invited him to visit, hoping that a change of scenery might help a bit. When there, he walked all the way up and down the Eiffel Tower – which at least wore him out. Since my husband and I had only a studio apartment, our landlady offered us a little room off a lovely courtyard which I considered much more charming than our grand building. It had been her husband's studio for writing and gave my brother some privacy, even if its attractiveness was probably lost on him at the time. My father, however, was not happy with us leaving my brother alone at night; he was extremely worried about his older son, whom he loved deeply, although the two of them did not always get along very well.

For a while, there were no more girlfriends for my brother – as far as I know. Then he married, i.e., *was* married, by a woman who, in my opinion, came nowhere near his earlier girls. She struck me as a manipulative and vulgar social climber who also managed to wrap

172

my father around her little finger. She and my brother had one son, but then she thought she had found somebody "better" and left – not for long. When she wanted to return to my brother, she exerted all the emotional pressure she could using the child to make him come back, but he had moved on. Ultimately, it was the child who suffered. At the time of the separation, he was too young to live with his father, who was often abroad, and Stefan had to attend a boarding school. I believe his mother wanted my brother to pay as much as possible emotionally and financially for not getting together again, for marrying another woman, and for starting a new family, but then, I do not feel charitable towards her and am probably not fair.

My nephew, who is also my godson, grew very tall and developed serious health problems that should have/could have been diagnosed earlier. He already has a second heart and will need a new one soon. My brother did what he could, took him on trips, paid for his education, and tried to include him in his new family, but over the years, Stefan had to learn to fend for himself and became a person who is not easy to get close to. However, for many years now, he has been an active and prominent member of Germany's Computer Chaos Club and is highly respected by his friends. . I watched him with one of them when they visited us in the US and on TV at the Club's big annual event, and I liked the way they treated each other with consideration, respect, and friendliness. Stefan has been to the US many times, visiting with us and attending meetings, but has become more and more critical of this country over the years. I wish I could have done more for him when he was younger, although I do not know what it could have been. The person who gave him unconditional love was my mother, his grandmother. He spent summer vacations with her and found warmth and belonging in her house.

New Friends

To return to my break-up with Fredy, it's safe to say that it hurt my pride and my trust in others and myself but forced me out of the comfortable and not-so-comfortable routines we had established and into meeting new people. It did not affect my life in what mattered most to me, my studies. I also continued rowing and coxing at the international meets. In winter, I went on ski weeks with the Austrian "Hochschülerschaft" [student organization], which offered affordable trips that were great fun. I still was not the best of skiers – the standards were quite high – but good enough to be invited by the various young men who were part of the group. There were fewer girls. We all had prodigious energy, skiing all day, going down to whatever village we were near to a five o'clock tea dance at one of the hotels, walking back up for dinner – we always stayed at places that were a bit out of the way and cheaper – and perhaps going back for dancing again or remaining in our lodgings and playing various parlor games.

I remember staying up all night one New Year's Eve and going skiing the next morning. I also saw some of the young men I met on these ski trips in Vienna. Two brothers, in particular, impressed me, not so much with their skiing but back in the city when we attended concerts. They came with the scores of whatever musical pieces were being played to read along. They were not showing off; it was what they normally did and what I could not do. I also joined a "Turnverein" [gymnastics club] in Floridsdorf. It was – and still is – customary to go for drinks afterwards. I was not fond of the drinking games, though, that were being played, such as "Whoever is born in January, get up, get up, drink up, drink up," and so forth through the calendar with repeats.

After Fredy, I decided that I would never allow a relationship to become serious if I was not in love, although I was still not sure what that meant and would feel like. All my reading had given me not so much romantic notions as the expectation of certainty. I followed through, going out with quite a few young men but not really becoming involved with any one of them. I recall a lovely boy from an aristocratic family who invited me to his parents' apartment in the castle of Schönbrunn – certain government employees could live there – to listen to Mozart's *Don Giovanni*, again and again, and him commenting on every nuance. We had the appropriate setting. Llanfranco – the unusual name stayed with me – had access to a car as well and invited me on exploratory trips he had researched, which were unusual. One time we climbed around in the ruins of an abandoned Trappist monastery somewhere along the Danube and imagined the lives of these long-gone monks, wondering if we could bear such an existence, although we were both drawn to contemplation. Many years later, I tried to find the place again, but never could, at least not for sure.

Another young man belonged to one of the many Austrian CV (Catholic) fraternities that regularly congregated in the entrance hall of the University. He was very conservative, like his fraternity. When I took him to a reading of Austrian dialect poets, such as H.C. Artmann, whose texts were often macabre and scatological, he was so shocked that he did not want to see me again. Another young man, Heinz, with whom I went out for some time, was a fellow student, kind, intelligent, and interested in everything that went on culturally in Vienna. He invited me to many avant-garde events, but also to some large balls in the city, which were held in the grand venues Vienna offers, such as the Imperial Castle, various palaces, and Vienna's *Konzerthaus*.

Most venues had more than one ballroom, each with its own orchestra, so you could dance to different kinds of music, including waltzes, polkas, and Jazz. I liked the old-fashioned quadrille, which usually took place before the midnight break and often ended in a raucous gallop, one couple holding on to the next, through all the rooms. Heinz had a scooter, so we could get around easily, and he could take me home after public transportation had stopped running. Between three and five in the morning, there was no place open in

Vienna where you could go and have a cup of coffee, except for the Café Havelka, which I am glad to say, still exists, even if, by now, Vienna has more establishments which are open all night. It may have also had them at the time, but they were not known by and accessible to young people like us.

Although I liked and respected Heinz very much and enjoyed going out with him, I followed my grand plan of not getting into an exclusive relationship with anybody with whom I was not really "in love." So, I broke things off when he appeared to become too serious. He did not understand my explanation, was hurt, and probably thought me eccentric. Soon after our separation, he received a Fulbright to the US. I saw him once more after his return when I was planning to go to the US myself to teach there and wanted to ask him for any advice he might have. Surprisingly, for an Austrian man, he warned me about the rude sexual behavior of male fraternity students in the US, which shocked him. He was an unusually decent guy, one who truly respected women.

My own experiences with American men were quite different from his warnings, though, but then I never attended undergraduate fraternity parties. While I was still living in Austria, I became friends with two young Americans. I met one at a gathering for Fulbright students in a castle in the Alps, where the Commission had arranged for new people from the US to meet Austrians, past and future Fulbrighters. I have no idea how I came to be invited because I was neither, perhaps because there were very few women that year. I found it a wonderful experience. From the Austrians who had come back, I learned, e.g., that it was customary in the US to start a lecture with a joke, then an alien concept to Austrian professors and something I could never learn to do comfortably, although I admired it in others. Among the many interesting boys I met on this retreat, there was a student from the Midwest who spent his year in Vienna and would become a faithful admirer and companion. He took me to the Opera, to concerts, and to many restaurants. I was not accustomed to the latter because we all spent whatever money we had on entertainment, high culture or low, not on restaurant meals. Most of us ate at home or cheaply in the student cafeteria, the *Mensa*. We just went for a coffee or a glass of wine in a Café. However, this young man, I do not recall his name, felt his Fulbright allowance was too much money, which he made a point of telling the Commission. Since he could not give it back, he spent quite a bit of it on me. However, he ate well too.

The other American I knew before I went to the US myself was more of a correspondent. I met him in London when I was in England doing research for my dissertation and trying to see as many sites and museums as possible. He followed me around in the British Museum and asked me to spend his last night in Europe with him, not in bed but wandering around the streets of London. It was a wonderful night; I still see us standing alone by the Thames, looking into its waters. He was on vacation from somewhere in California. Upon his return, he sent me many letters and photographs about his life, his apartment, and his roadster, all of which intrigued me. I wrote back but do not know for how long. My mother was concerned that I would promise him all kinds of things – as she put it – fearing that I would go meet him in the US. Ironically, and to her disappointment, I eventually married an American and left Austria.

University

It was a matter of course in my mind that I would go to university, although, in 1955, this was still not very common for girls. The attitude of many families was that a girl would marry soon. If she went to school until age eighteen, she would be considered well-educated and a suitable wife for any middle or upper-middle-class man. She could bridge the time until her wedding by taking a white-collar job to keep busy until then and to earn extra money for her trousseau. If she kept working as a married woman, she would certainly stop when she had children. In the period between World War I and World War II, traditional expectations had been loosened, but after 1945, they held sway again for a while, even if or also because many women had lost their "breadwinners" and had no choice but to work to support themselves and their children. However, this was not considered worthy of admiration but rather of pity.

Besides, although students did not have to pay tuition to go to university and in Vienna could even live at home, making university study considerably cheaper than in the US, there was the issue of lost income. Why study and forgo the money you might be making if your degree did not lead to anything? Men needed advanced degrees to gain advanced positions and would eventually catch up when women would be long gone from the workforce. Even my brother, who had to work hard at the *Technische Hochschule* [the Technical University of Vienna] to earn his advanced degree, sometimes felt that this took too long and that there were faster ways to become an engineer and earn a good income, if not a *Diplom Ingenieur* (Dipl. Ing.) with the steep career open to one. My father, rightly, never questioned the time it would take him but was skeptical about me, although my goal was quite practical and feasible. I wanted to become a "professor" in the fields I loved, German and English, and teach at a *Realgymnasium*. This was one of the few professions readily accessible to women – if they were lucky or well-connected enough to obtain a position. Also, it did not require you to give up work when you had a child – and a mother or somebody else helping you.

In addition to sharing the general skepticism about girls attending university, my father held a gendered view of the professions. Eventually, he accepted that I would study to become a "professor" if I insisted on it. However, he did not allow my younger brother to pursue the same route. Putzi wanted to become a "professor" as well and chose mathematics and sports, but my father said no, that was no profession for a man. My younger brother had to attend the Technical University and obtain an advanced engineering degree, like his older sibling. The consequence, which my father never lived to see, was that Putzi did not complete his studies. He became one of the perennial students of which there were many at the time. Eventually, though, he turned a part-time job at Austria's two major magazines, *Profil* and *Trend,* one general, the other business, into a full-time editorial job. It was interesting work, paid well, and turned him from a mediocre student into a superbly well-informed, knowledgeable man. Would his life have been different if he had followed his original choice? He was such a genuinely nice person that he would have done well in education, been popular with his pupils, and perhaps, become a school principal somewhere.

As a "professor," he would have received an adequate, if smaller, salary but would have been a tenured civil servant with a substantial pension. And he could not have been let go as my brother was after the magazines were bought by a large German conglomerate, a merger he had fought as an elected representative of the employees' association. This was a blow that forced him into early retirement and affected him deeply. Yet, I doubt he regretted the course of his life and the work he did. In general, the decision between becoming a civil servant – there were many more at the time – or going into private enterprise faced young middle-class Austrians joining the workforce then and still does, with many opting for the security of government work with its perks. The entrepreneurial spirit was not highly developed nor highly prized when my brothers and I grew up, although there were and now, again, are quite a few Austrians who founded innovative businesses and made names for themselves internationally, but finding success abroad was/is essential. Without this international recognition, it was/is hard for you or your product to do well in Austria.

While my father was not enthusiastic about my attending university, he did not forbid it. Perhaps he hoped that it would take me away from Fredy. Where was my mother in all of this? She did not voice any objection or doubt and just supported me in her own way. When I came home in the early afternoon, she always had a warm meal for me, never mind that family dinner was in the evening. And she patiently helped me shop for materials for dresses, which she then made for me. This meant that I always had well-fitting, good-looking clothes. She did not ask for much assistance around the house, although she had more than enough work with the family and the gardens she continued to maintain. After my grandfather's death, we eventually sublet the vineyard for some of the grapes we still pressed. Yet there was enough left to do.

During the summer, my brother and I had to help a bit with picking fruit. Whatever we did not use from the harvest or can ourselves, my mother continued to sell for extra income. Nobody came to pick up the fruit anymore, so we had to cart it ourselves to big truckers who had started up in the area and took it to the markets in Vienna. This task fell to my brother and me. We hated it because the people we had to deal with were rough and treated us with condescension even though, in our naïve arrogance, we thought getting an education made us special. They did not care. They were becoming wealthy, enlarged and renovated their houses, bought big cars, etc. Studying and learning were not highly prized in our rural surroundings. Yet, over the years, some of these people paid me for lessons to their children so they could do well enough in school and go on to advanced secondary education, which would prepare them better for business and give them some prestige. The times were changing as more people began to do well for themselves materially. I noticed this in my little business that brought me pupils from Bisamberg, Floridsdorf, and downtown Vienna who came from increasingly diverse backgrounds. Many parents, although now well-off, did not have the time nor the education to help their kids. I usually succeeded in getting my charges through the next exam and to the next grade and saw many different households in the process, some quite poor, where – often – the mother desperately wanted her child to have a chance at a better life and some nouveau riche, where the parents wished for their offspring to get every advantage possible. I did not take too many pupils, though, just enough to cover my needs, which were modest since my parents housed and fed me. I took this for granted, so my pride in my financial independence was not as well-founded as I thought. Still, not having to ask for money gave me self-confidence and the expectation that I would never want or have to in the future.

When I started university, I was not yet eighteen and at a loss about what to do. Advising for incoming students did not exist, and I knew nobody who started out at the same time. The person I turned to was my former principal, who could not help me either, except for telling me to relax and sign up for fewer courses. The subjects I chose were English and German literature. The former, because of my earlier trip to England and the impression the America House in Linz had left on me, and the latter because I had learned to love it.

Getting to the University of Vienna – then entirely on the Ringstraße – took me a minimum of one hour each way on public transportation. Normally, I went every day and again regretted the lost apartment, which would have been within walking distance. However, the long commute did not dampen my enthusiasm. I could read on the bus and on the tram. It was hard, though, to go back and forth more than once in a day. So, I had to stay in town all day if I planned on an event in the evening, which I frequently did since I wanted to do, see, and hear as much as I possibly could. Besides going to the British Council and the Vienna America House during the day (although the latter struck me as much less interesting than the one in Linz), I attended new plays, performances, and concerts at night. When I was still with Fredy, I made him take me to things in the evening; later, I went with other friends. I continued to love the Burgtheater, which remained quite conservative: Bertolt Brecht, e.g., was not yet acceptable. Still, I saw most of the established German playwrights and many international authors in translation in wonderful productions and with great actors whose past was still not talked about by anybody I knew. At best, we received mixed messages about a kind of integration/reconciliation.

One example that stayed with me was a wonderful staging of the 19th-century playwright Ferdinand Raimund, who was quintessentially and safely Austrian and "untainted" even if the actors were not. What made this performance especially memorable was the scenery designed by Oskar Kokoschka, with the stage floor constructed as one of his landscapes in relief. Kokoschka had been an *enfant terrible* in the early twentieth century, had gone into exile, and was now internationally famous and proudly hailed in Austria.

Another very different but even more unforgettable production had nothing to do with the German past, at least not directly. It was the British director, Peter Brook's, and his ensemble's stunning *Titus Andronicus*. Vivien Leigh, Laurence Olivier, and Anthony Quayle came to Vienna and performed this Shakespeare play, which was rarely, if ever, seen on German language stages, although Shakespeare in translation was the most popular playwright then and may still be. They, of course, used the original language. Peter Brook's production did nothing to tone down the play's cruelty, on the contrary. Still, because of the deep impression this staging made on me, I later, when I lived in the US, moved heaven and earth to see Peter Weiss' *Marat/Sade* on Broadway under Brook's equally outstanding direction. By then, my husband and I were students in New Haven, Connecticut, where my love of theater was only surpassed by his, and we went far and wide to see exciting performances, a practice we continued throughout our life together. Of the many superb stagings I have seen, Peter Brook's were the most memorable. *Titus Andronicus* gave me a first taste of what an outstanding director could do for a text. From then on, I became quite sensitive to that potential and the many mistakes directors could make by being too "far out" or traditional, but the latter always irked me more.

The Burgtheater

Very often, I spent all day, and a good part of the night, in Vienna and came home on the last bus, which left Floridsdorf at 12:30. I waited for it by myself because friends from Vienna, who had accompanied me that far, needed to get back home on public transport as well, few had cars or scooters. Still, it never entered my mind to be scared even when – sometimes drunk – men tried to pick me up. Perhaps I was lucky, but I do believe Vienna was quite safe then and is so even now, at least in the areas I frequented. I should add that not all my activities in Vienna involved "high culture," many an evening was spent dancing or talking in a café, but I always returned home.

During the day, when I was not attending lectures and seminars or going about town tutoring, I often walked from the university to the National Library and worked in its reading room. It was a thirty-minute walk which I always enjoyed very much, although the high-heeled shoes I insisted on wearing started hurting after a while. My route took me through the center of Vienna, the first district, where grand old buildings and churches are crowded together and the streets narrow. You had to peek into doorways and see the inner courtyards to appreciate the magnificence of the old palaces which lined the street along Herrengasse [Master's Lane], which I took for part of the way. Most buildings in downtown Vienna also go very deep down into basements and cellars, which I sometimes saw because many were and still are being used for events such as readings and lectures.

The Austrian National Library is part of the Imperial Palace complex, where a grand library was among the baroque additions designed by Fischer von Erlach. Its façade goes onto the Josefsplatz, a beautiful square bordered on its other sides by the gothic Augustinian Church, where the hearts of the Habsburg emperors are buried, separate from their bodies. Facing the library façade are two "modest" palaces. In the center of the square stands the statue of Emperor Joseph II, Austria's one enlightened monarch. The entrance to the reading room was an inconspicuous little door in the grand façade. Patrons came to a small hallway with a telephone booth, a cloakroom, and a tiny toilet. From there, a lovely staircase led up to the magnificent "Prunksaal" [ceremonial room] of the library whose door you passed on the way to the much more modest, but comfortably old-fashioned, reading room.

The door to the "Prunksaal" was always open, so I could, and often did, throw a quick look at its splendor. It contained statues and glass cases and was lined by two stories of leather- and gold-bound volumes and domed by a stunningly painted ceiling. I have always admired those grand baroque libraries, this one, and those in Austria's large monasteries, such as Melk. Books were prized possessions for the monks and status symbols for imperial and aristocratic houses. When I was growing up, they were also proudly on display in the households I knew, but always in bookcases, never on open shelves, which made them even more enticing to me. Perhaps my continued love of libraries is inspired by my youthful impressions. Ownership of books was highly valued, no matter how grandly or modestly displayed. Hence, my sadness about the loss in significance that the collection and possession of books has suffered.

"Prunksaal" [Stateroom] of The Austrian National Library

The holdings of the National Library in Vienna continue to grow, though, because every book published in Austria must be held there, and many rooms in the big complex of the Imperial Castle are being used for storage. Nowadays, there is storage elsewhere as well as digitization. When I was a student, the books you ordered were retrieved by employees who carried them on their backs in wooden crates through halls and up and down stairs. One time, I was permitted to follow a librarian into this "hinterland" and was so fascinated that I toyed with the idea of becoming a librarian myself. The actual librarians then had doctorates, but as an ordinary user, you only encountered one of them if you had a special question or needed something unusual. Mostly, we dealt with lowly and sometimes grouchy employees. Nowadays, by the way, my beloved National Library is very different. It still has a vast staff of many ranks, who are friendlier than I remember, perhaps because I am no longer a student. Now there is an enormous modern reading room that stretches along the side tract of the "new" addition to the Imperial Palace, which was never really used except to provide a balcony for Hitler to greet the cheering Viennese on the Heldenplatz in front.

Contemporary Reading Room of The Austrian National Library

Despite its size, this large reading room nowadays is often very crowded, which was rarely the case with the comparatively tiny one I used as a student. Now, there are many additional rooms of varying functions and computer stations with access to the fully digitized catalog; laptop connections abound everywhere. A large lounge with newspapers and vending machines and a cafeteria in the basement – all amenities we could only dream of when I was a student – make working easy and pleasant.

I wonder, though, if much has changed in the ways readers get the material they need. You must still order what you want and wait. There is no possibility of going into the stacks and looking around, something I always enjoy doing in US libraries. I suspect you would get lost in the Austrian National Library or be shut in by mistake. This happened to me once when I was doing research in one of its catalogs in an even older building. I had no cell phone then and spent a desperate hour shouting down to a deserted square from a high window. As for taking books home from the National and University Library, that was not an option for students.

When I visited Vienna in recent years, I was struck by how much libraries have changed. First, there are so many more students, and then there are all the electronic innovations. In my days, the University Library still had a catalog room with enormous handwritten volumes which listed books that had appeared before 1932 – in *Korrent* [German script], no less. For books published after 1932, we had card catalogs with typewritten and handwritten entries. More than anything, what strikes me when I think about my years as a student in the second half of the fifties, is how small-scale everything still was then. People carried on and settled into what had gone on before the "Hitler interlude," it was reconstruction as restoration and higher education was still reserved for a privileged few. Yet, with all the striking modernizations and mass access to higher education nowadays, I have the impression that habits and attitudes have not changed that much.

My cohort took our privileged positions for granted, however modest they were in terms of ease and comfort compared to today. But the young people I see these days still exude entitlement, in fact rather more so than less. Yet, I am also sure that there are many among them who are socially, politically, and environmentally much more aware and active than we were. We cared deeply about culture but scoffed at politics, which in Austria then was one of collaboration between the two major parties, the "blacks" (ÖVP, the People's Party – conservative) and the "reds" (SPÖ – Social Democrats). There was also an FPÖ which, as has been mentioned, consisted of former Nazis and now attracts new ones. For many of the young people during my time, political affiliation, mostly the parents', only mattered because it helped them get a job. Good positions in Civil Service were handed out proportionally, depending on which party, red or black, had received more votes. Eventually, everybody would be taken care of. We were not very concerned about social inequities because most people were still relatively poor and trying to catch up on material possessions, including housing, furniture, and then cars. This happened quickly, and differences soon became more pronounced and noticeable again, but we thought that they did not matter that much. I am talking about material differences because, socially, the divide between the solid middle and upper middle class on the one hand and the lower middle and working class on the other was even more pronounced then. However, money was not yet decisive in this divide. We did not have much but did not feel defined by our possessions. When I say "we," I mean myself, my family, and the young people around me. I knew my own parents needed to be careful, but they did not talk and certainly did not fight about money. As mentioned, my father voted for the Social Democrats, the party supposedly watching out for working-class interests, but that was the extent of his social commitment to the "lower classes."

Besides, the Social Democrats represented all those who did not care for the "People's Party" and its closeness to the Catholic Church. As for myself, tutoring made me aware of social differences, and looking back, I can say that, with it, I helped my poorer students, but I did not do it for free; that never entered my mind. And I – as well as my cohort – believed that postwar Austria was building up a social network that evened out economic inequality and poverty. It did, to a limited degree, so that the differences are not quite so egregious as they are in the US. Later, I studied Marxist ideas and sympathized with them. However, I did so globally and abstractly, not with reference to Austria.

My cohort and I also thought that we were open to and interested in the larger world, but that meant Europe and the West. Although fear of THE bomb and a Third World War was more acute than it was in later years, we did not really talk about it – until the Hungarian Uprising of 1956, when newly independent Austria, which had pledged neutrality to gain this independence, was caught in a difficult in-between position. Hungary was right next door. Its capital was only 133 miles from Vienna, the border, the Iron Curtain, even closer. Our sympathies, officially and privately, were with the revolutionaries, but for the government, any breach of neutrality was dangerous because it might disturb a very delicate balance. When Soviet tanks eventually crushed the uprising in Hungary, people in Austria feared that they might roll right on to Vienna and/or that any defense on the part of the West would lead to a nuclear war. (All that sounds familiar at this moment with regards the Ukraine.) Little Austria handled the situation as well as it could by providing humanitarian aid and by welcoming refugees from the short-lived reformist government of Imre Nagy.

We talked about our fears and welcomed the refugees, but that was it. When the status quo was re-established at the expense of the Hungarians who had fought for change, we all settled down again in the shadow of the Iron Curtain and the arms race, which had already produced the H-bomb. We felt helpless, wished for calm, and preferred talking about other things like art, literature, music, and – with many – sports.

The great worry of today – somehow the proliferation of nuclear weapons despite arms treaties has been accepted as a given – global warming and the degradation of the environment did not concern us. My brother, I, and many of our friends felt close to nature, the cultivated nature of our farming environment in Bisamberg, and what I thought was "wild" nature along the Danube and in the woods of our little mountain. And we loved skiing or hiking in the Alps. We did not think skiing was destructive, but then, exploiting Austria's natural beauty through its all-important tourism industry was just beginning.

Klaus and me Skiing in the Alps

Everything was still comparatively small-scale. My nostalgia for the idyllic places of my childhood and youth continues to increase my present and selfish disgust at the crowds of tourists and vacationers in all the areas I remember as quietly beautiful. When I came back later to ski in the Alps with my sons and brothers, I had the strong sense that we were encroaching upon places high up in the mountains where we had no business being, although lifts had taken us there. There was nothing but these lifts, a few human beings, and snow-covered peaks all around us – as well as a hut somewhere nearby with good food and drink. The situation struck me as eerie. Yet, I was there.

Besides the ever-expanding exploitation of nature through tourism, Austria's hybris was the gigantic hydroelectric plant of Kaprun, where the massive reservoir submerged large areas and the dam's construction cost many lives, especially under the Nazis when forced labor was used. During my youth, Kaprun was celebrated as a great feat of engineering. It was, of course, and made Austria less dependent on fossil fuels. Ironically, the name Kaprun is also associated with a terrible disaster that happened many years later. A fire killed 155 skiers on the funicular, taking people through a tunnel up to the glacier of Kaprun, where they could ski year-round. I never wanted to ski on a glacier, but I knew and admired enough people who did. Now, I regret my past insouciance concerning the environment and support the young people who worry about and actively fight global warming and its dire consequences.

Professors at the University

I loved my studies, although my professors overall were anything but scintillating. Siegfried Korninger was an exception. He was in charge of the English American Institute and easily filled our largest hall, the Auditorium Maximum, with his lectures. I enjoyed them and took notes assiduously, but sometimes, after a ball night, my head drooped, and my hand produced scribbles even with him. Korninger introduced us to English playwrights of the 16th and 17th centuries, such as Christopher Marlowe, John Ford, and Thomas Middleton, of whom we had never heard and whom he and then we found fascinating. He also taught us about English Romantic poetry, some of which I still know by heart. He was relatively young and the only one of my professors at the University who had never been a Nazi. He had spent a semester in Texas but had held on to his prized British accent. And he left American literature as well as modernism to visiting professors, most of them sponsored by Fulbright. I recall one who introduced us to Faulkner's *As I Lay Dying* AND James Joyce's *Ulysses* in one semester. My English then was by no means up to these books. Nevertheless, they impressed me deeply so that I remember them more vividly than many others, which I read more easily and faster. Korninger was the only professor in English, but besides the visitors, he had assistants and lecturers who took care of a variety of other subjects, from Old English to Grammar.

German was the top discipline in the humanities and thus had three chaired professors, each with a different area of expertise – and each with his own variety of a Nazi past about which none of us students knew anything; I certainly did not. Only now, when I googled them

191

to make sure that I spelled their names correctly, did I find out. Hans Rupprich held the chair in "newer" German literature, which meant from the early Renaissance into the 19th century. His specialty was the Renaissance, but I recall his lectures on Goethe and Schiller, albeit not fondly. They were extremely boring because he read them, literally, in a monotone no less, probably from the manuscripts to his books of which he wrote many, though I never checked. The content and text of the lectures did not vary; thus, you could buy mimeographed versions from the student association. I wonder why I even attended, perhaps out of eagerness or because I did not want to buy the notes. When I looked up Rupprich on Wikipedia, I found a cautiously worded entry that he had been a Nazi functionary and, for that reason, did not receive the chair in Graz for which he was being considered in 1946. In 1951, however, he was called to the more prestigious professorship in Vienna, where he had a highly respected career, his past quickly forgotten.

Moriz Enzinger held the newly created chair for Austrian literature, for which his colleagues had chosen him without political input, which was unusual at the time, and, I believe, still is. His lectures were no more exciting than Rupprich's, yet I liked him much better. Somehow, he communicated the sense that he deeply cared for the writers and texts he presented. He was an expert on Adalbert Stifter and did much for the recognition of this great Austrian prose writer. A kind of "positivist," Enzinger discussed everybody who had contributed to Austrian literature, including women and did not classify them by "importance" – no canon for him. When feminists began discovering unknown female authors, I had already encountered those from Austria in his lectures. Enzinger joined the NSDAP early in his career when he was a professor at the University of Innsbruck, perhaps for his own protection, I now naively think – he was a hunchback. Right after the War, he was removed from his post but only briefly. Soon thereafter, he received the prestigious call to Vienna.

The third German professor, who did Medieval Studies, then still the most highly regarded field in *Germanistik* – as well as the most used and misused for nationalist purposes – was Dietrich Kralik. He came from a well-known family of intellectuals and of the three professors in German Studies, was the most invested in National Socialism, having been an avowed Antisemite long before the *Anschluss*. After the war, he, too, was briefly suspended but quickly returned to his chair. He was an expert on the *Nibelungenlied*, Germany's – and Austria's – much-studied national epic. I still remember his small seminar where each student was assigned one stanza, which we had to analyze linguistically, historically, and literarily. It was a very good exercise, even if we did not have nearly enough students for the many stanzas in the epic. I enjoyed the close readings we did.

Neither Kralik nor the other professors communicated obvious Nazi ideology or antisemitic opinions in their teaching, i.e., I did not perceive anything, but I would only have noticed the most egregious examples. What strikes and even shocks me now, is how quickly their publicly acknowledged support of National Socialism was forgotten and buried. Whatever views they themselves may still have held, in their teaching and writing, they had moved into the perceived neutrality of textual criticism and the accumulation of biographical and historical facts. Would they have had to be kept on and even promoted, or would there have been others to take their place after the War? Probably yes, but not many. A great number of the younger people had been killed on the front and may have been even more dedicated National Socialists. After all, Josef Goebbels had a doctorate in German literature; moreover, most of the people who reinstated and promoted my professors had little problem with their past.

The "End"

As much as I loved my studies, I had no intention of drawing them out beyond the minimal four years. The requirements, when I finally figured them out, were stricter for the teaching certificate than for the doctorate, which was less regulated. In matriculation, we had all received a "Studienbuch," a booklet in which the courses for which we signed up were recorded. We then obtained our instructors' signatures at the beginning and at the end of the semester, attesting to the fact that we had attended their lectures. Nobody checked, however, to ensure we had done so. We were supposed to take a few examinations on some lecture courses of our choice, pass a certain number of proseminars and seminars, and write a dissertation for the doctorate and a long essay for the teaching certificate. For the latter, we also had to take rather difficult written examinations.

If we passed all the requirements for the teaching certificate, we could become instructors on the secondary level, at a Realgymnasium, or equivalent college prep school, and – after a trial period as an assistant teacher – become "professors." Besides this practical training at a school, no pedagogical preparation was offered or expected. I assume things have changed in the meantime. The doctorate was even less rigidly bureaucratic, although the final examinations are called "rigorosum" making you expect strict interrogation. There is not just one, as the Latin suggests. They are oral and consist of a series of examinations with professors who are relevant to the individual student's interests and previous work. At the time, they were held in the privacy of an office or even a home, as had always been the custom. Numbers were still small enough. Most students who planned on teaching did not bother with a doctorate; only those who hoped for other careers, such as journalism and publishing, or wished to go as far in education as they possibly could, went for it. The title of Dr., which in Austria – and Germany – always precedes the name as the standard form of address, signals that you are an "academic."

In Austria, titles, including the Masters, are important, especially since all inherited aristocratic distinctions were abolished after World War I. Still, Austrians love titles. One can argue that academic titles are, at least, earned – except when they are being used to address the wives of title holders, as was still the norm when I grew up. I find it funny that the owner of our grocery store in Bisamberg, who greeted her female customers with every conceivable title owed to the husband, did not address me as Frau Doktor even though, being a relative of my mother's, she had sent me a congratulatory card when I received my doctorate. She had known me since I was a little girl, and, in her worldview, women acquired valid titles through marriage.

As for university careers, a dissertation and doctorate were only the first steps to becoming a professor, and I knew of nobody who aspired to that goal, certainly no woman. However, there was a female professor who lived in Bisamberg, a theologian whom everybody considered an eccentric person, although I could not see what made her one, except that she was not married, kept large dogs, lived with her sister in a big house – and was a female university professor.

I finished my dissertation and the requisite substantial paper for the teaching certificate in good time. This meant I could take all my exams in one semester, on the assumption that this bundling would be more efficient since most of the material was the same and involved cramming. I knew I would forget much of it if I spaced things too far apart. What I did and do remember, though, were the many original texts I had read during my four years of study. I had gone around to the antiquarian bookstores in Vienna, of which there were many, to buy complete editions of the well-known and not-so-well-known writers of the past. Most were still printed in old German script. Irrespective of and frequently despite the dry lectures from my German professors, I continued to love German literature and learned to appreciate English and American prose and poetry. Contemporary German or English-language books were a little harder to come by simply because they were more expensive than antiquarian ones, but Vienna had many bookstores where affordable paperbacks were available, including books in English. I spent most of the money I made from tutoring on books and on clothes, i.e., on expensive material from which my mother made clothes for me. I did not need much for entertainment because it was not yet customary to go Dutch with a young man, at least not among the ones I knew.

Enzinger's emphasis on Austrian literature, as distinct from German, and Korninger's introductions to the Anglo-American traditions provided different perspectives and kept me from an overly Germanic orientation in my studies. I chose to write my dissertation with Korninger on a topic he assigned: "Charakterisierungskunst in den Romanen der Mrs. Gaskell" [The Art of Characterization in the novels of Mrs. Gaskell]. It had to be written in German. My topic was removed from the subjects on which this professor normally lectured and took me into a new world, that of woman writers and the 19th-century English novel. I had never heard of Elizabeth Gaskell and wonder now if Korninger was in the forefront of her slow rediscovery which much later blossomed into well-known BBC TV productions, such as *North and South* and *Cranford*. Elisabeth Gaskell had been the wife of a Unitarian Minister in Manchester and knew and wrote about industrial life in England as well as the small-town gentility in which she had grown up. And she concentrated on women, including working class girls, and even chose a "fallen woman" as a main character. In the process of my research, I also read up on theories of the novel, as usual, much more widely than I needed to. And I went to Manchester to work in the Gaskell archive there.

I stayed at a YWCA with English girls who worked in town, the first and only time I ever lived with other young women. Unusually, I was the only transient at this YWCA, and I appreciated getting to know my housemates. I also liked English food, in contrast to most people from the continent. At the YWCA, I loved breakfast, high tea, which was served in late afternoons on the weekend, and most of all, evening tea-time. Every weekday, around nine p.m., we all gathered in the kitchen where crackers, jam, and tea were laid out. We laughed and chatted – and I gained a few pounds.

At these get-togethers, I learned much about the lives of the other girls, about their boyfriends and their dreams of marrying soon, dreams which I did not share. They all impressed me as intelligent women, but most of them only seemed to care how they would spend their weekends and with whom. When they left the house, they were well dressed and carefully made up, but I was shocked when I visited their rooms. They were a mess. The YWCA and the Gaskell archive were in nice neighborhoods, so I had little occasion to go to the poorer areas of the city, yet I was, again, taken aback by the overall grime, as I had been in Preston. I could not believe the dirty trench coats that otherwise well-dressed people wore on public transportation. This all sounds as though I was obsessed with order and cleanliness, and perhaps by some standards, I was/am, but I consider myself messy enough.

The few less-than-positive impressions I had gotten did not spoil my enjoyment of this lengthy stay in England, though, which I also used to make longer visits to Wales and to Stratford on Avon, where I saw all the plays on offer that season. The manager of the youth hostel there even made an exception for me to stay longer than the three nights normally allowed. Of the other places I visited, the one which impressed me the most was Cambridge, which I found to be incredibly beautiful with its combination of green lawns, gothic buildings, and the water of the Cam. It appeared idyllic and peaceful, much more so than Oxford with its bustle and traffic. On later visits to Cambridge, when I could no longer wander freely through the colleges, I was disappointed by the noisy traffic.

I also spent time in London and assiduously looked up all the buildings, museums, and galleries I knew from my reading. The British Museum was simply overwhelming, the Victoria and Albert Museum a big ugliness, the Tate Gallery wonderfully eye-opening. Altogether, I tried to take in more of London than I possibly could absorb. Along the way, I stayed in YWCAs or in Youth Hostels. For food, I usually relied on breakfast and tea, but eating was not a priority; seeing was. I felt perfectly happy going around by myself, but occasionally struck up friendships, so with a young US-American woman who was much more sophisticated and worldly than I and who took me along to one or two Soho restaurants where we had dinner with friends of hers, new or old I did not know. I remember though her teaching me that I should never wear the same outfit twice in a row, but always alternate, advice I have followed ever since. When I returned to England and London later, which I did several times, I was always a little bit disappointed not only with Cambridge, but generally so, because my experiences never came up to the intensity of this trip which I made by myself.

My dissertation was acceptable and accepted, but nothing special. I did not return to it, except very recently, when I was asked to write a short biographical entry on Mrs. Gaskell. When it came time for the "rigorosum," the most important part fell to Korninger, with whom I apparently did very well because he told the whole Auditorium Maximum how good an exam it had been. I was not at the lecture then and had to be told by others.

Still, I missed receiving my doctorate "sub auspiciis praesidentis" as I would have liked, because I had gotten a grade of 2 (the equivalent of a B) on one seminar paper or exam, while I had to have all 1s (As), including the final report from the *Realgymnasium*. I told no one, however, that I would have liked to receive this special distinction, which was a continuation or, better, a restart from the times of the Austro-Hungarian Empire when it was called "sub auspciis imperatoris." And I was sensible enough to acknowledge to myself that it did not really matter, still...

The degree was a Dr. Phil., so there were additional in-person exams with two philosophers or one philosopher and one psychologist. I chose the latter option and had a psychology professor who expected us to know – and buy – the latest version of his book, something I considered to be shabby blackmail. I refused but passed the perfunctory examination anyway. All told, it left no impression. For philosophy, I had to visit Professor Leo Gabriel in his home. He was closely involved with Austro-Fascism and had been a full professor since 1951. Still, as usual, I knew nothing about him personally, only that he would examine me on his special and Catholic version of existential philosophy on which I read up. I had to go to his apartment, where he greeted me amiably and told me that he had just come home from a night out. He was still in very good spirits but not at all hung over.

After we had talked some – it did not strike me as an examination – he claimed to be very impressed by me and predicted that I was slated for great things. He was still in a very good mood. I remember little or nothing of his ideas even though I later studied the French Existentialists and wrote a *rororo monograph* on Simone de Beauvoir. By then, I had forgotten Gabriel altogether. Maybe at the time, what impressed the jovial professor was not my thinking and knowledge so much as my appearance. I was quite young and wore my special exam outfit, which was attractive but not sexy and which my mother had made for me. I should add that neither Gabriel nor any of the other professors whom I saw one-on-one ever made advances. Still, I wonder when this holdover from earlier times of going individually to professors' houses ended. In the past, the number of students was small, and the candidates were only male. Now, I have no idea how things are being handled.

There was one occasion, though, when one of my examining professors was underwhelmed. It was also an in-person exam – for the teaching certificate – with Moriz Enzinger. He had assigned me the required major paper – on "Hermann Bahr and Adalbert Stifter" – for which I did original research in the manuscripts collection of the National Library. I remember my visits there fondly, sitting alone in a room whose windows looked out onto one of the many courtyards of the Imperial Palace where the Lippizan horses of the Spanish Riding School partook in their morning practice. (I believe they still do.) Watching these beautiful animals going through their paces provided a distraction and an extra bonus to my work.

Enzinger liked my paper and even recommended publication, something I never thought about until I came to the US and began teaching at the college/university level. Under the title "Hermann Bahr und die konservative Revolution" [Hermann Bahr and the Conservative Revolution], it then became my first publication in a prestigious European journal. However, my performance on the oral exam did not impress Enzinger at all. He asked me questions about writers from the turn of the last century like Hugo von Hofmannsthal, whom he had never taught and whom, at the time, I only knew superficially. The University did not teach living or even recently dead authors. Still, Enzinger rightly expected us/me to have read more widely than what he taught in his lectures, including relatively new literature.

Although this strong – albeit never exclusive – emphasis on study and research might sound boring, it was not at all for me. I loved it and wanted to do as well as I could, even if the grades, including the "sub auspiciis" distinction, did not really matter. I knew that I would go into teaching when I finished my studies and counted on my former principal to help me get an appointment, as he had promised. At the time, you needed some connections – and you probably still do.

Yet, while a student I occasionally toyed with the idea of learning additional things and getting different jobs. One summer, I worked as a receptionist for the most popular Austrian cartoonist, who called himself "Ironimus" and was also a well-known architect. Despite his caricatures, he was a gentle and kind man, something which cannot be said of his friend Gerhard Bronner who hired me – at least not so easily. He had a biting tongue and, among many things, was a well-known cabaret performer and writer who worked in the cabaret, "Brettl vorm Kopf" [literally: Board in front of the Head], together with Helmut Qualtinger and others. It criticized

Austria and Austrians, and they loved it. Personally, Bronner's behavior could be abrasive as well. Once, as a guest in his bar called "Marietta," where he occasionally sat at the piano, I heard him greet a couple with the remark: "Welcome! The gentleman has excellent taste, the lady less so." The poor guest slunk to his table. In the limited interactions I had with Bronner, who appeared to manage his friend's exhibition in the "Künnstlerhaus," he was always friendly and kind, though. I enjoyed working for both men who stopped by regularly.

At one point, I also took a secretarial course to learn typing and stenography. I remember one of the instructors being interested in me and claiming to admire my ability to spell correctly – it was better at the time than it is now – and recommending that I join the Foreign Service. I did not seriously consider this option, but I am glad I learned to type properly without looking at the keyboard. I felt this way, despite the fact that young women then were told to avoid acquiring those skills so they would not be tempted or pushed into secretarial jobs. Yet, knowing how to type well turned out to be very useful to me then and even more so when we began using computers.

Indeed, looking back, I feel that everything I studied, learned, and did as a child and young woman, perhaps except for stenography and speed reading, benefited me in some way. I only regretted what I did not pursue, like piano playing beyond the most rudimentary level. Yet, I never considered myself sufficiently well-informed and well-prepared. I was and remained naïve and felt that others were more mature, more in command, and overall better. That feeling has never left me no matter how old I became and how much I accomplished. Perhaps though, this constant sense of insufficiency has kept me curious and wishing to learn new things.

As I reflect on my life, I feel lucky about my postwar childhood and youth, which spared me wars and provided an ambiance of trust in renewal and improvement, although I did not reflect upon this at the time. My early years were much easier than my parents' after World War I, and thus, I cannot blame them for the choices they made and from which they suffered. They provided me and my brothers with as safe and protected an environment as they could in which to grow up – in a country that for a long time did not reflect on its problematic past. I am not saying that this cocoon was good; I had to move away, "out of Bisamberg" and out of Austria, to gain a wider, more critical perspective, but I have no right to blame my parents for accepting National Socialism as so many of my generation did theirs. It was for me to use the opportunities they never had and to grow intellectually and emotionally. Did I have to move away geographically as far as I did? Perhaps for me yes, although my brothers and many in Austria eventually became more critical as well. However, I have to admit that neither I nor my generation, be it in Austria or the US, used our reprieve from major catastrophes well enough to secure a safe future for our children and grandchildren.

For me, moving away came about serendipitously and quickly. After the "Sponsion," the small ceremony officially conferring the doctorate – there are no big graduations –my former principal made good on his promise and sent me to a friend of his in the Ministry of Education, who offered me a teaching position. It was not in Vienna but in a small town in Lower Austria to which I could easily commute from Bisamberg. My father was very pleased and offered to help me get a car so I could continue living at home. Finally, his driving lessons would bear fruit – they had been painful enough for him since the driving test was the only examination I ever failed.

My father had worked hard to make me a more skillful driver than I had the talent to be and even harder to have me understand how a motor worked, knowledge on which we were tested as well. I passed the dreaded driving and technical parts of the exam. But then, there were also traffic rules and regulations, and these I flunked ignominiously, not because I had not studied for them but because the examiner wanted to have his fun by putting me, a young Frau

Doktor, down. He asked me how many babies you could put into a VW bus. I fell into the trap of his absurd question and said as many as I wished, or it could hold. However, there was a law which set the limit at eight heads, no matter how small. My stupid response sufficed to send me home without a license. I was angry and my father ten times more so, but I repeated the test and passed.

It turned out that I did not need a driver's license quite yet because, out of the blue, my plans changed. A former fellow student of Korninger's showed up at the University looking for somebody to teach German at her College in the Midwest of the USA. He recommended me, and I was excited to go – for a year, I thought. I talked to my sponsor in the Ministry and received his promise that he would hold my position or assign me another one when I came back. I did return, but only to get married to the man I met in the US sitting at the desk next to mine in the communal office of the Language Department of Monmouth College. He had an MA in French and planned to stay a year as well. Then he would go on for his Ph.D., but only one US university, Yale, which was considered the best in his field, would suffice. However, this is his story which I will tell separately. For me, the upshot was that we got married, lived in Paris for a year, and then moved to the US.

The settings for our wedding ceremonies provided an amusing contrast. In Austria, you had to have a civil marriage certificate for the wedding to count; a church ceremony was optional. When we finally had all the necessary stamps and papers – not an easy process in France – we were civilly married in the grand town hall of the 18th district behind the Champs Elysée because we stayed nearby at a small hotel. At home, we married in the modest wooden church in a nearby village where I had held my Lutheran children's group meetings. Both my brothers and at least one cousin would later use it as well. In church, I had a small wardrobe mishap that could have turned into a big one, but at the time, it did not register with me, although I could not forget it later. My mother had designed my wedding dress, which had little handmade buttons run all down the back. During the ceremony, they slowly came undone with just one last button holding things together. I did not notice anything and wondered what my mother was doing at my back right after the minister had finished. Nobody said anything except for my brother, who told me with his characteristic grin that everybody had stared at this last button. My mother must have been mortified, she had taken so much trouble with my gown, but she did not say anything either after she had finished buttoning me up, something I did not even notice. It was not customary then to have enormous weddings, just family and very close friends were invited to a sit-down dinner. More people came to the church, and I was pleased that my former principal showed up and that my father invited him to join us for the meal.

Wedding with Laurence

As much as I held on to my family and Bisamberg in future years, I never regretted my choice of partner, the decision to leave, and our life together. It was so much more varied, interesting, and open to change than what it could have been in Austria. My childhood and youth there were wonderful and formative, but my life in the US with my husband, my children, my additional studies, and my career opportunities made me grow and understand so much more than I ever envisioned possible. And it made me finally realize that my happy childhood existed on top of and next to enormous suffering about which I had no idea then and which, despite all my reading, I still cannot fathom, as I do not really delve into everything going on around me right now. However, I know much – too much for a happy old age. Not that my generation in Vienna and Austria did not change as well or that my life in the US was as questioning, open-minded, and charitable as it could have/should have been, but I kept (and still keep) learning more and doing more than I would have if I had stayed in my accustomed surroundings. I had the best of two worlds and am grateful for that. Did I do enough for others and the future of the earth? Definitely not, but I did strive to make my students think critically and raise my sons to become good, kind, and open-minded men – or, more likely, they just followed their father's example.

Laurence

His mother called him Laurence Jr. and would have liked for him to name his first son Laurence III. He did not wish to go that far, but always insisted that he be called by his full name, Laurence, never Larry. Indeed, he refused to use abbreviations for anybody in the family. It was never 'Andy' or 'Chris' for his sons Andreas and Christian. However, he had a wealth of nicknames for all of us, such as "the fellow" for his older son and "the Rick" for the younger, and "Bé-Bé for me, not Baby.

I believe his insistence on full names was left over from the southern formality, which had expressed itself in his mother's preference for Laurence III; she was not a pompous or snobbish woman. With him, remnants of formality manifested themselves in other ways as well. He erased every bit of his regional accent from his English, insisted on learning standard French, not the French patois of his Louisiana relatives and neighbors whom he nevertheless liked and enjoyed. It was not snobbishness on his part either, more a matter of respect for others by using their full names and for language by wanting to speak "properly." His writing was somewhat formal as well. When he helped me with my essays and papers in English, I was never happy with the result. And Christian's English teacher always knew that he had helped and asked that he stop – of course.

The culture in which Laurence grew up was illiterate. Neither his mother nor his father could read or write, yet they managed very well in their small rural Louisiana community, business, and household. His mother was an intelligent woman, slim and always well-dressed. She designed the family's two houses, both following the changing trends of the area, with the last in beautiful old brick. Then she helped her daughters plan theirs. Yet, she suffered from not being able to read or write and hid the fact carefully from her neighbors. When Laurence encouraged her to take courses to learn, she was so afraid somebody would find out that she refused. Both parents were respected members of the community, though, the father was even beloved. He was not bothered by the fact that he could not read or write, perhaps because he was always busy working, enjoyed what he was doing, and knew what tools to buy and what to do when it came to practical things.

At first, his partner, later his oldest son, helped him with the ever-increasing paperwork around the business. What he loved was telling stories which he did better than most people in his oral culture, where this was a prized skill. He did it with much laughter and good will. His good will extended to black people as well, although he was a strict segregationist. Still, he appreciated the local African Americans' – albeit separate – ways. Discussing his attitude with him, which I tried a few times, proved useless and only made him obstinate and angry, so Laurence and I avoided the subject. Besides, his church and priests confirmed his opinions.

He was illegitimate. He knew it, of course, and made no secret of the fact, but it was not talked about. The only thing his biological father gave him was the name Romero, but there was never any contact, although he did not live far away. Laurence Jr. must have known but never talked about it; only his youngest sister brought it up many years later. The mother had found a husband quickly and then had born ten more children. Once during a visit, Laurence Jr. and I drove around the countryside and visited a rice farm that had been turned into a museum with the former owners' pictures on the walls – all Romeros. We told Laurence Sr. about our discovery and wondered if they were relatives. He said nothing. Perhaps he knew more, perhaps not. Later, we speculated if one of those men in the pictures might have been his biological father.

The stepfather was harsh and cruel, beating the child and working him to exhaustion, cutting sugar cane and doing chores. There was no question of school, but then his half-brothers and -sisters did not attend school either. At thirteen, Laurence Sr. left the family with his mother's consent, but he had to promise to stay in touch with her, which he did faithfully into her old age. He moved in with a kind couple, who had no children and needed a helper, but eventually sent him to barber school. From then on, he took care of himself, opening a shop together with a friend, getting married and supporting a good-sized family, guaranteeing college for all his children, although only Laurence Jr. went. Despite his tough childhood, he became a genial, fun-loving adult who gathered the larger family around him for frequent barbecues. He did not bear grudges and was friendly with everybody, even his stepfather. All this was told to me by his youngest daughter, Sheila, who loved her father very much, not by Laurence, who only talked about the paternal and genial side of his father and probably did not even know about the terrible childhood. Laurence Sr. did not speak about it unless you kept asking, as his youngest daughter did.

When the family celebrated his 80th birthday – nobody knew when exactly it was, Parish records had burnt, but a date was set and used – Laurence and I wanted to join them, but he asked us to come later when he and we had more time to spend together. So, we did and visited with him and Sheila in Houston, where she lived. He clearly enjoyed himself and kept telling amusing stories about life in his small town and his many relatives and friends. I also remember a trip to Galveston, where I rented a horse-drawn carriage for us to ride around in. This did not turn out to be the special treat I thought it would be. He told me afterward that he had had more than enough rides in carriages, it was nothing special, and I was wasting my money. He was not at all interested in touristy activities. When he visited with us in Winchester in the Boston area, he usually stayed back from sightseeing trips but went for daily walks in the area around our house and immediately befriended other elderly men from the neighborhood whom we had seen regularly but did not know at all.

Soon after our get-together, he died. We went to the funeral, and the wake, which was my first in the US; it struck me as a big party

208

with an open coffin in its midst. Sheila sat next to the coffin, stroking her dead father's embalmed face; the others mingled, chatted, and drank coffee. Although I had never seen them, I recognized all the people from Laurence Sr.'s stories. They had been presented so vividly that there was no mistaking who was who.

Laurence Sr., whom they called Peewee because of his small size, was an avid gardener, supposedly waking up at three in the morning to tend to his vegetables, and a skilled hobby carpenter. He had a well-equipped workshop in his backyard where he made all kinds of furniture. One of his good friends was the local dentist who credited him with saving his life by preventing him from drinking too much and committing suicide. One of Peewee's specialties was gun cabinets, which were displayed prominently in many a living room in the area, including in his sons-in-laws'. He himself did not own one, had no guns, and did not hunt, but he liked making those prized pieces of furniture for others. Stories have it that the actor Paul Newman saw one at a friend's house and asked to have a copy made for himself. Peewee had no idea who Paul Newman was, but his daughters did and were very excited, hoping to meet the handsome actor. I do not think they did.

Laurence Jr. was not interested in gardening and did not inherit his father's skills in carpentry. Indeed, he was singularly inept. When he tried to do the smallest thing, he made a mess of it, swore a lot at the time, and laughed at himself afterwards. However, he did inherit the gift of storytelling even if he revered the written word. As a child, he had to go to a neighbor's house to read a newspaper or look at a magazine. As an adult, he could not live without his *New York Times* or, when we were abroad, the European edition of *The Herald*, which still existed then, preferably both. His great love was literature, which became his profession. He taught French and French literature, but in his research and writing, he branched out to other cultures as well. For pleasure, which is the wrong word because he enjoyed it all, he kept up on contemporary American writers. I remember him chuckling next to me over *Portnoy's*

Complaint, which I did not find quite so amusing. I believe we have most first edition paperbacks of the major US writers who came out in the sixties, seventies, eighties, and early nineties – slowly crumbling. Laurence also loved film and theater, with the latter very much an acquired taste because, in his youth, there was no theater for him. However, there were films, and he described those he had seen and liked with so much enthusiasm that watching them on his recommendation was always a letdown, even if they were very good movies. I specifically remember *The African Queen,* which disappointed me when I finally saw it.

Laurence did not talk much about his childhood, not because he did not want to – there were occasional amusing episodes – but because he thought there was not that much to tell. And he did not reflect on what made him want to become a professor and intellectual, a totally different course from his sibling, cousins, and childhood friends. There were many, and he was anything but an outsider among them. Indeed, I believe his childhood was "happy," but I think it was not content. He wanted more, not money but wider horizons. His mother, a farmer's daughter with twelve brothers and sisters and three half-siblings, supported him; he was her second son and favorite.

———

Lucille Baronet and Laurence Romero Sr, Laurence's Parents, with Andreas

By Catholic Louisiana's standards, their own family was relatively small. Besides an older brother, there were three girls. Laurence loved his oldest and youngest sister very much but had a distant relationship with his brother, who never married and continued to live at home. Everybody thought he was rich because he was frugal and supposedly even miserly, but never with Andreas and Christian. Gil, short for Gillard, became very ill, although he was something of a "health nut," and in his last years, was bent over and in pain from severe osteoporosis. He finally bought a gun and shot himself. The day before, he called Andreas and Christian as he sometimes did, but without saying a formal goodbye. He did ask for their social security numbers, though, which I found strange. Still, we had no idea about his plans. He left his siblings quite a bit of money, wishing, I now find, that Laurence's share would go to his children because Laurence was no longer alive then. However, a lawyer informed us that according to the Code Napoleon, which regulated

211

such things in Louisiana, Andreas, and Christian could not inherit their father's portion. I wanted to at least ask about this law, but neither boy wanted me to pursue the question, so I let it be. They were concerned about their aunts' and cousins' feelings. Just recently, I discovered that this was probably fraud on the part of a brother-in-law who took over the administration of the estate and used one of his lawyer friends to write the letter. The others trusted him, as Laurence would have done. He liked this brother-in-law very much and spoke highly of him. Anyway, it was a long time ago, and this relative is no longer alive.

The few stories Laurence told about his childhood and youth were of having to mow the lawn, which he hated to do and often got to at the very last minute or even forgot, making his normally easygoing father angry. He also described extended family barbecues with mounds of crayfish, shrimp, steaks, sausages, and all kinds of Cajun food, such as shrimp or crayfish-étouffée, at which his mother was an expert. She was an excellent cook and kept a very clean house. I remember being struck by the fact that towels were only used once, a habit that Laurence kept and passed on to his sons. One story that stayed with me was of the time before air conditioning was introduced when he sometimes slept on the bedroom floor because it was cooler. Their first house was raised on bricks, as was the custom in the area then, so air circulated underneath – and also snakes and other critters, which did not bother Laurence but spooked my imagination. However, the family had air conditioning right when it became available.

Laurence hated all sports and refused to learn to swim. When his mother sent him to swimming lessons, he conveniently kept losing his bathing trunks. Only as an adult did he finally make a concerted effort to learn and arrive at keeping himself afloat. Later, in the family, we also played tennis as a vacation sport. When the children and I went alpine skiing, he tried to cross country. At dinner afterwards, his stories about mishaps and adventures were much more colorful and amusing than ours. He did not just fall; he was snorkeling in the snow. In Boston, he became a Celtics fan and watched games with our former babysitter and friend Edith and Christian. There was invariably much excitement and shouting about the Boston team, the Celtics, which was very good then and won championships.

Despite Laurence's dislike for most sports – he did a bit of hunting, which is considered a "sport" and very popular in Louisiana – he was well-liked in school and was elected president of his High School class. He would have become valedictorian as well if there had not been an "interloper," as he jokingly called the girl who joined his school and class late but got even better grades than he. He did not mind and received some other distinctions, but none of that was as important to him as moving on, first to a small area college and then to Louisiana State University, where he obtained his BA and his Masters in French.

At that time, language study was much in demand, and an MA was good enough to find positions at the college level. Laurence then left Louisiana for good and went to Monmouth College in the Midwest to teach French. That is where we met, and he wooed me with his stories and reading poetry to me, not always the best, though. I remember Rudyard Kipling was a mainstay, but at the time, I was enthralled because I had fond memories of a story by Kipling, which was in my English school book. It told about a mongoose and his enemies, the snakes, Nag and Nagina: *Rikki Tikki-Tavi*. What also impressed me was the fact that Laurence was not possessive and could not be easily manipulated like earlier boyfriends. Once, he refused to take me to a football game that I wanted to see – at least one, I begged. When I threatened that I would go with somebody else, he said, "Fine," and meant it.

Laurence's plan was to earn some money and then go on for a Ph.D. in French, but only one University interested him, Yale, which supposedly had the best French Department in the US. Its faculty consisted entirely of Frenchmen, except for Victor Brombert, a

Russian Jew born in Germany but educated in France. During World War II, Brombert belonged to the so-called Ritchie Boys, a special unit of young immigrant men with good German and other language skills who wished to contribute to the US war effort and were used for intelligence gathering and interrogating German prisoners after the Normandy landing. The War was, by no means, over yet, and their work quite dangerous. As far as I know, nobody among the students at Yale was aware of Brombert's past. He never talked about his distinguished non-academic career, and we students considered him prissy. The other French professors were also outstanding men, and not only as scholars – there were no women.

From Monmouth, Laurence wrote to Henri Peyre, the chair of the Yale Department and doyen of French studies in the US, to ask about applying. Peyre's response was prompt and handwritten. It said that he needed to spend time in France before he could be considered. Money was an issue, though; there were no readily available scholarships for somebody already teaching. However, luck intervened. At a teacher-student conference in Monmouth, Laurence met a guest of the wealthy father of one of his students, Prince Murat. At the time, that is all I learned about this French aristocrat and benefactor, and I doubt that Laurence knew much more. Now, checking on Google, I find that it must have been Joachim Louis Napoléon Murat, 8th Prince Murat, who had close ties to the US. In conversation with father and guest, Laurence talked about his plans, and the prince offered to hire him as a translator for his Paris Office – with a full salary for half a day's work. And he followed through on his grand gesture. At the end of the academic year, Laurence could leave Monmouth College for Paris – quite a change. He and other friends had complained constantly about the dullness of the Midwest, where a trip to Peoria was a highlight and Chicago urban sophistication itself. I, on the other hand, enjoyed my time in Monmouth. Everything was new for me. Yet, I was ready to go to Paris with Laurence, and get married there in a civil ceremony which would be followed by a church wedding in Austria with my family. There was never any talk of Laurence's family attending at the time. To them, Europe was very far away. However, his mother and father were happy for him and welcoming to me. It turned out that getting the necessary papers for a civil wedding in Paris was a bureaucratic nightmare. It would have been anyway, but at the time, government offices were being overrun by the many people from North Africa whom the Algerian War had dislocated. However, unlike most of the others with whom we stood in long lines, our situation was not desperate, and we eventually managed.

In Paris, Laurence found an apartment in the heart of Montparnasse, on Boulevard Raspail, in a house built by Le Corbusier. Our landlady was the widow of a writer and lived nearby in an older apartment typical of the area – on two floors. Our place was not too far from the Sorbonne, where all our classes were being held. The walk there was beautiful, if relatively long, and took you through the Jardin de Luxembourg. The apartment building in which we lived had a narrow road frontage but courtyards that went far back. Our large studio covered the width of the building and had windows all along one side, which gave out onto the first courtyard.

Across from us, there was a painter's studio that covered two floors. We never met the painter, but we saw a lot of him and he of us. There were, of course, curtains, but during the day, we kept them open. Our place was designed for a – male – bachelor and had a small entry, an enormous living/dining/bedroom, a large bathroom, and a tiny kitchen, which was not meant for preparing big meals. Yet, although I was not much of a cook, I found it easy enough in Paris to put excellent dinners on the table. Laurence always made breakfast. Later, he would cook frequently and well, but then, I had more leisure than he did. It was the only time in our married life that I did not contribute to our budget. I only took French courses.

However, soon in our relationship, I learned that he was not good with money and took over the management of whatever we had. Not that he was a great spendthrift, he just did not care about money. He liked having his newspapers, books, tickets to the theater and the movies, and occasional restaurant meals, but otherwise, he was quite frugal and had to be pushed to buy new clothes, for example. However, he never kept track of the cash in his pockets and often ran out. This was a problem when credit cards were not yet common. One time, he took me to a very good French restaurant in Chicago, but when it came to paying, he had to lean over the table and ask to borrow some money. For a short while, his never knowing how much cash he had made me angry, but then I learned to be sure that I always carried enough with me and that we obtained an American Express Card right after we became married, although for some time to come and hard to imagine now, many smaller places did not accept credit cards, so you had to be prepared. Ironically – and sadly – he was very provident when it came to retirement savings which were made easy for college professors. He took full advantage of them and contributed the maximum, only to never profit from any.

In Paris, Laurence's office was near Place Clichy, a very different area of Paris from where we lived, less bourgeois and intellectual than Montparnasse but quite interesting and lively. I have no idea what kind of business was being transacted in the office where he worked; we never talked about it. It must have demanded a lot of translation because Laurence made a good friend, Claude, a Frenchman who had served as a soldier in World War II. He was married with a family and worked as a full-time translator. Perhaps there were others as well. The two of them often went to lunch together in one of the small restaurants around Place Clichy, where I occasionally joined them. Sometimes, additional people from the office came along as well, but nobody ever talked about work, and I did not ask about it. I was intrigued by little things, e.g., the fact that in the restaurants where we ate, customers had their own cloth napkins with their differing napkin rings to be reused for the week. The salaries people were paid must have been sufficient because Claude, whom we visited a few times at his home, could support his family adequately. Of course, the two of us had enough as well. We both enjoyed Claude's company and laughed about his descriptions of the German food he was served in his prisoner of war days, including the "Knödel" (big dumplings), which he called "boule" with all the contempt he could put into the word.

Laurence took a variety of courses at the Sorbonne, but what the year in France gave him – and me – was exposure to French culture as it manifested itself at the time. There was everyday life in Paris, and there were the various famous sites on weekends which we researched and visited assiduously and repeatedly, such as Versailles, Fontainebleau, and the castles in the Loire Valley around which we made a bicycle tour to which we invited my younger brother. It was a gorgeous trip on which we did more good eating than strenuous biking.

It was also a great time for theater with many excellent directors and actors. The movement to reach out to a broader public and eventually to the banlieu, the districts on the margins of Paris, was just beginning. Laurence also liked the TNP (Thèâtre Nationale Populaire), then still under Jean Vilar and playing in the Palais de Chaillot. Vilar tried all kinds of methods, such as low prices, to make his a truly popular theater, from which we profited. He also produced German playwrights like Kleist, Büchner, and Brecht, which Laurence discovered, as did I. At the time, they were not played much in Vienna. The French made them relevant and interesting again to the German-speaking public. Geographically closer to our apartment was the Thèâtre de l'Odeon, then under Jean-Louis Barrault, which played Paul Claudel, whom Laurence liked very much, and Ionesco. It was less readily affordable, but we attended it anyway, as well as so many other theaters among the incredible choice we had, including the Comédie Française, which struck us as venerable but a bit dusty – at least it did me, perhaps because my French was not good enough to appreciate the subtleties of Racine, Corneille, or Molière. For Laurence, these productions, although, or more likely, because they were, for the most part, traditional, may have laid a seed for his dissertation topic, which was still far off. In addition to the theater, all the little cinemas in town allowed us to see new and old films in French, German, and English. There was even a cinema, "The Raspail," in our building.

It must have been in the late fall or around Christmas when Laurence formally applied to Yale; I lived on my Paris cloud and only became aware that he had done so when one day in spring, he set an especially nice breakfast table and leaned a letter against my coffee cup. This would become his habit for any good news or nice surprise. It was his acceptance, including a scholarship that meant paid tuition and a stipend to live on. I do not know if he had ever worried, I had not, and we had certainly not spent any time talking about the possibility that he might be rejected. However, from then on, we could enjoy the remaining time in Paris even more fully and without any subconscious worry whatsoever. Towards the end of our stay, my parents came to pick us up and drove us back to Vienna with some detours – I remember Amsterdam. I also recall that it was a stressful journey; my mother and I were accustomed to giving in to my father, but Laurence was not, although, normally, the two men got along well enough.

At the time, it was still common – and cheaper – to travel across the Atlantic by boat, so we did. Besides, we had two big steamer trunks with things we had acquired, including wedding presents and my trousseau, which consisted of dishes, linen, etc. All that was a bit much for our first year in New Haven, where Laurence and I lived among other students – in a large room with a private bath in the Yale International House on Prospect Street. The House was set up for graduate students, some from the US and some from abroad, although the international mingling was only superficial. Our contact with the foreign students in the house broke off after the year, while some of the US students became life-long friends. I was a foreigner as well, but somehow, that did not count. All the American– and Canadian – students eventually had outstanding careers, such as professors at MIT, Yale, and elsewhere, lawyers, and university presidents, so I wonder what happened to the foreign students who returned to their countries, e.g., to Africa. They probably did very well too. However, I never heard from or about them.

The hub of the International House was its large kitchen, where everybody had a cupboard and refrigerator space and prepared their own meals. Among the inhabitants was a handsome Sikh who cooked up a storm of Indian food and then left his many pots in our large industrial sink. He was probably accustomed to servants cleaning up for him – if he had ever cooked before. When he did not listen to our entreaties to clean up after himself and the situation got out of hand, we decided to hire a cleaning lady rather than get into fights.

For most in the house, the cooking was less ambitious; the discussions were not. They ranged far and wide in politics, philosophy, literature, and the arts and were infused with the kind of optimism and trust in the future that characterized our generation then. Laurence and I were one of two couples in the house; the other was from Iceland. There were also the host or house manager, a former Yale undergraduate, who was now studying medicine, and his wife. They gave a sherry party every week, which appeared to be the extent of their responsibilities. Beyond the three married women, who were "just wives," there was one female graduate student from France; all the others were young men.

During the year, I tried to earn a little additional money by typing a Yale-German professor's book – it was in German – worked for a Chemistry professor as a part-time assistant, albeit not in the laboratory, and taught German classes at Albertus Magnus, a local Catholic College. I also decided to become a student again and applied to the Yale Program in Comparative Literature, which was quite small and quite selective. I already had a doctorate in English and German, so acceptance – with a scholarship – was a bit easier. However, I was not the only person in the program who had an advanced degree; most of the others did as well. I also began teaching German language in the German Program at Yale. In addition, both Laurence and I earned some extra money by giving courses in German and French, respectively, at Southern Connecticut State College.

Thus, we were quite comfortable financially and could even pick up a Volkswagen in Wolfsburg, drive it in Europe, and then ship it to the US. In New Haven, the problem was parking, though. Even if the basement apartment we rented after the International House – everybody, except the manager, could only stay a year – was close to the Yale campus, we could not resist taking the car nearer to classes and promptly received many a parking ticket. A few times, our VW was towed to some distant lot from where we had to bail it out – at considerable cost.

In the last few years in New Haven, we rented an apartment in a new housing development on Dixwell Avenue in the town's black area which was close to the University. It was supposed to help integrate the town and proved a good experience for us – I doubt though that it ultimately helped integration. We had nice quarters with two bedrooms – just in time for Andreas, born in 1966. There was even a tiny backyard. The size of the apartments in the development varied. Next to us, we had a family with five children with whom we became good friends.

Not only by moving into this housing development, where other graduate students followed us but also by having a baby, Laurence and I started a trend. I was the first to attend seminars with a large belly, and I remember the Dean of Yale College and a professor of French taking me aside after his class and telling me that I should not interrupt or stop my studies. It would be a shame. His remark surprised me because he had always struck me as a man's man.

Indeed he was; later, I found out that he had fought in World War II on the French as well as the US side. However, he turned out to be one who respected women and was a good model for his then-still-exclusively male undergraduates.

Laurence and I took and passed our Comprehensive Exams the same year, I believe. There were no dissertation fellowships, so he immediately applied for a teaching position. The plan was that wherever he received an offer, I would see if a job was available for me as well, and we would go there. At the time, jobs in Foreign Languages and Literature Departments were still plentiful, an effect of the Sputnik Era. I believe Laurence had six or seven offers from very good universities and chose the University of North Carolina in Chapel Hill because there was teaching for me at Duke University nearby – as a lecturer in German. We rented a large house from Duke a few steps away from the Women's Campus, where I was assigned an office. The men's campus at Duke was connected by a shuttle bus, and classes were scheduled fifteen minutes apart so students and instructors could go back and forth through the large, beautiful grounds. There was no distinction anymore between the women's and men's classes and faculties.

Laurence commuted by car to Chapel Hill. In the fall, winter, and spring, Duke was a beautiful park. In the summer, we fled the sweltering heat and went to Europe and to Vermont. We came to Durham with one small child, and while there, I gave birth to Christian in 1969. There was no maternity leave at the time, so I took only three days off from teaching. My students wondered. To help us with the children and the house, we hired au pair girls whom family and friends in Vienna recommended. Rosi, the first, stayed for two years, then Edith came. She made the move from Durham to the Boston area with us and worked for two years as our au pair. Then she returned to Austria but no longer liked it there and came back to study in this country, eventually becoming a professor here. The children and Laurence liked her very much, and I did too.

We still had dissertations to write. Laurence had chosen a topic in theater with Jacques Guicharnaud – on modern stagings of Molière. It later became a good and even useful book. Years afterward, at a performance at the ART (American Repertory Theater) in Cambridge, a dramaturg told me and a friend, who was also a dramaturg and a theater director in Berlin, that Laurence's book had helped him considerably when he was preparing his production of a Molière play – I do not recall which one. However, writing this dissertation, which demanded a great deal of research, took longer than the three years allowed by the University of North Carolina, so Laurence's contract was not renewed.

He had befriended a well-established faculty member at Duke who was also the chair of its French Department and wanted to hire him, but this plan suddenly fell apart. Apparently, the fact that Laurence had accompanied me earlier to a dean at Duke to try to negotiate a conversion of my position as a lecturer into that of an Assistant Professor was held against him. The discussion about my request had been amicable if unsuccessful, but he was told by his "friend" that we had committed some unpardonable crime – I still do not know which – and that all talk of Laurence coming to Duke had to be dropped.

Neither of us had liked Durham, Duke, or Chapel Hill anyway. As graduate students, we had enjoyed a stimulating intellectual atmosphere at Yale, now, we felt that there was nothing but snobbery and racism, which were more noticeable at Duke but existed at both universities. Although Laurence came from the deep South, he did not like the heat in summertime either, not to speak of the racism and the narrow-minded atmosphere among most of our colleagues who, at parties, were only interested in gossip and chitchat – we thought. In the town of Durham, segregation was even part of the topography. One block had nice, large houses and paved streets. The next, small, shabby ones on rutted dirt roads so that the help could live close by.

Looking back, I realize that Yale was not integrated either, but some of the graduate students as well as the town of New Haven, i.e., its mayor at the time, tried to work against segregation. I must say that fresh out of an excellent graduate school, Laurence and I were quite arrogant intellectually and in our sense of being socially progressive. In Durham and Chapel Hill, we looked down on the people around us who did not appear to even think about change. Duke considered itself the Harvard of the South and perhaps still does. However, then, this applied to its societal standing, not its academic might. The latter eventually changed, but I must say that even at the time, I had very good students – all white – and I enjoyed teaching them. Two of them I saw again much later. One had become a professor of German, the other wanted me to meet his son.

We also received some interesting visitors, among them Marcel Reich-Ranicky, Germany's long-time star literary critic. Laurence and I hosted him, and Laurence, who by then spoke good German, showed him around the Duke Gardens and told many stories. Reich-Ranicky was so impressed by them that he advised him to write fiction and forget about academic books.

When Laurence had to find a new appointment, we wanted to move up north again. Although he had grown up in the south, he liked life in New England better, the atmosphere and the climate. By then, we were part-owners of a simple farmhouse in Vermont and spent parts of summers when we were not in Europe there, although, originally, it was winter and skiing which had attracted me. Laurence played along. We bought the house together with a friend from Yale while we were still graduate students. The friend's father ran a Christmas tree business and knew about land and farms for sale. Laurence jokingly called him "my agent," but I think the New England gentleman did not appreciate this appellation. We did not pay a bank for the mortgage we, of course, needed, but the farmer's wife. This arrangement helped her to have a yearly income. And it was good for us because we were still students when we made the purchase and would probably have had a hard time at a bank.

Soon, Laurence and I became sole owners of the house but kept most of the adjoining land in common with our friend. During the academic year, we rented the place to students from the Center for Northern Studies, which another friend nearby had founded. It would have been too expensive for us to maintain during the winter. There was one problem, though: the students we rented out to were all great young women and men, but having these outdoorsy people in an old house was a disaster that angered Laurence every spring when we came back. Motorcycle maintenance was not a good idea of what to do in a country kitchen. Yet, we loved Vermont and the house, and the children did as well. Still, we never considered moving to rural Vermont for good.

In the three years we had spent in the South, teaching positions had become much harder to find. Eventually, Laurence received an offer from Tufts University in Medford near Boston. He was happy to be in an urban area and closer to our Vermont house, which had also become somewhat easier to reach because of the new highways being built. However, at first, I could only get part-time teaching at Emmanuel College in downtown Boston. However, Laurence, unfortunately, and unfairly, did not receive tenure (a permanent appointment) from Tufts. At the same time Emmanuel offered me a full-time job, Tufts did the same. I took the latter. Yet, Laurence and I never taught there together. It was a difficult time. He had to move again and eventually joined the faculty at Villanova University near Philadelphia. We stayed in the Boston area, though, and Laurence commuted again, this time by plane and much further – for the rest of his life. At two and a half years, Christian had become ill with childhood Leukemia, and we needed Boston's Children's Hospital, his best, then still a slim chance for survival. I continued to teach at Tufts University, where I eventually received tenure.

For many years Laurence had an excellent teaching schedule at Villanova. It allowed him to be gone for no more than three days in the middle of the week. The rest he could spend with us. In addition, there were holidays as well as winter and summer vacations. He did not accept any administrative duties, such as chairing his Modern Languages Department, which would cut into time with the family. Still, while all this sounds and was quite feasible, it couldn't have been pleasant for him to live in rented rooms when he was away from home. He never maintained an apartment and never complained but had a few stories about his various landlords or - ladies and his flights back and forth. One of his "hosts" was a former Polish aristocrat and a drunkard, another the typical Main-Line lady. For several years Laurence was lucky and rented from an elderly couple, the Bachmanns, whom he liked very much. Mrs. Bachmann was an avid gardener. She had studied horticulture with Mrs. Barnes, wife of the founder of the famous Barnes art collection and knew both Mr. and Mrs. Barnes well. She was the only person I ever knew who kept a social register close by. What interested Laurence was that she was knowledgeable about the culture on the Main Line and that she was a good cook and provided excellent company. She loved a good story as much as he did.

Laurence spent all the time he could with his sons and was a loving father. Of course, they would have to speak for themselves. There was a lot of teasing and laughing. When they were smaller, he sat with them, reading and acting out the Asterix and Obelix series, of which we had copies in French, English, and German. He was also very involved in their schooling and always took care of staying in contact with their teachers on all levels, but especially in grade school, when they went to Buckingham in Cambridge and, later, to Junior High in Winchester.

Until he was 16, Andreas celebrated his birthday – on the 5th of July – in Vermont. He had good friends up there but also invited some from the Boston area. Then Laurence demonstrated his love for his son most selflessly: After the traditional birthday party, he took the boys, usually six of them, for overnight camping to a cabin in the woods by Wolcott Pond. It was Andreas' wish, and Laurence granted it, although he detested the camping, the cooking by the fire, the late nights, and the early mornings, not to speak of the discomfort of sleeping bags and schlepping everything in and out again. I do not remember when these outings started and when they stopped, but they went on for quite a few years.

As already mentioned, carpentry was also something that Laurence disliked and was not good at. Yet, together with George Nash, a carpenter of the kind which Laurence described as guys – most common in Vermont – who simply slapped a nail bag around their waist and called themselves carpenters, he put wooden shingles on our house. George was one of the many hippies who then flocked to Vermont. He had a college degree and even some training, if not as a carpenter, then as a roofer. When he came in the morning, Laurence served him a big breakfast. Then, the work proceeded with much joking and laughing. They also built a lovely screened-in porch, which had one fatal flaw: it heaved up and down every winter. No attempt at remedying the situation, even the most desperate measures, helped, such as when Laurence rented a truck and tried to use it to pull out one of the concrete posts and major culprits. The result was a crooked post and a porch that continued to heave. Supposedly, Laurence and George had dug as deep as was prescribed for posts but not deep enough. This flaw remained a constant source of frustration. Still, the porch provided an enjoyable space for mosquito-free family meals, crowded little parties, and quiet reading.

The openness Laurence showed about doing things he did not really like to please his family, also held for things he did enjoy. Then this openness enlarged his perspective. He was curious and, in his all too short life, grew considerably intellectually as well as in his tastes – no more Kipling for him but Emily Dickinson, Langston Hughes, and Sylvia Plath. His master's thesis was on a now mostly forgotten French poet and playwright of the early 20th century, Charles

Vildrac. I do not know if he selected the topic himself or if it was assigned. He assesses the man fairly but does not make any big claims about him and his importance.

When it came to the dissertation, his choice was more ambitious and fell upon one of the greats of French theater, Molière, and modern stagings of his plays, with Jacques Guicharnaud as thesis advisor. It took Laurence some time to write and finish it, but it was a daunting topic and not so easy to do besides teaching and family. Also, different sources, in addition to libraries and books, were needed. After reworking, the dissertation became a book that was well received – as such books go, and as has already been mentioned.

In terms of academic type casting, he was now a specialist on the classical period of French literature, which included Racine and Corneille, but dealing with modern theater productions turned his interests to contemporary writers, especially Jean Marie Koltès, a fascinating avant-garde playwright whom we saw performed in Paris, Strasbourg, and Vienna. And Laurence also pursued a much larger project as a follow-up on the Molière book: A study of modern theater productions of the "classics," not just French, but English and German as well. It was very ambitious. He became extremely well-read in theory, and we had good excuses to attend theaters all over, in Germany, Austria, and France. The later seventies, eighties, and nineties brought forth many great and innovative theater directors. Eventually, Laurence would have had to limit the scope of his study and make a judicious selection. I do not know how he would have completed this project had he been given the chance. It was exciting, though, because, as he argued, only inspired contemporary productions could keep important playwrights of the past alive and relevant. It was also an undertaking that brought Laurence more and more into the European cultural sphere, because theater does not really play a large role in the US, certainly not classical plays.

We often talked about these issues and did not always agree. Indeed, we rarely did, but life with Laurence was stimulating and fun for me. We could have had many more good years and a great retirement, as they say, but that was not to be. He developed a disease called myelodysplastic syndrome. Although in 1996, when it was diagnosed, he was in an age group for which a bone marrow transplant, which offered chances at a cure, was already considered risky treatment, he decided on this option for which his youngest sister Sheila served as a donor. The other choice would have been frequent blood transfusions, but he did not want to live as an invalid. Everything appeared to go well, and he was even sent home with a healthcare company supposedly providing the needed skilled nursing. They did not, forgetting to renew his infusion during the night, which triggered a whole sequence of events that ultimately led to his death. He became completely dehydrated and had to be transported back to the hospital. I remember that one of the men coming to pick him up had a cold.

At first, there was no bed available in the special Bone-Marrow-Transplant ward at the New England Medical Center, where he had been. When finally admitted there, he came down with a respiratory infection which got worse quickly. Where on that trajectory and how he had picked it up, I never knew. It was the kind that is relatively harmless for most people but very dangerous to babies and immune-compromised adults. When breathing became difficult, I was with him all night, hoping that something could be done for him in the morning. By then, he was scared. Despite an oxygen mask, he could hardly speak, but at one point stammered that he was going to die, which I tried to deny, at another, that love was important. These were his last words. In the morning, he was intubated and moved to the Intensive Care Unit, where he remained for a few days on life support. Then we were told that they had to shut the system down. There was no chance for him; his whole body had given up. We hung on as long as we could but eventually had to agree.

After twenty-six years, I still ask myself how long he was conscious and what he suffered. When Laurence was being intubated, Christian was there and had the presence of mind to ask him to squeeze his hand, which he did. Then, however, it seems that he lost consciousness. I hope he did. I sat with him, played some music, and, from time to time, told him I loved him, but I do not believe he was aware of anything any longer. I was in shock and, to a certain degree, still am after those many years, always wondering what mistakes I made and what I could/should have done differently.

I do know that the home health service was at fault and that I might have sued them for negligence, but that was not something I had the strength to do. Moreover, it would not have helped him. I should have insisted that he stay in the hospital longer or that the men who transported him wear masks. But then his doctor told me that this was the first time that he had that respiratory infection on his ward, so he may have picked it up there. While Laurence was in the hospital, I was with him all the time and only went home to sleep, yet I feel I left him alone and did not talk to him enough about important things while I sat at his bedside. I was numb and hoping to plow through things, never expecting them to end the way they did. I am still haunted by the idea that I was not as good to him as I should have been and ask myself if he was as happy as he deserved to be. He was a good man, a very good man. Many people seem to have liked him very much. This I just realized when, after twenty-six years, I looked through all the correspondence he had received while in the hospital. At the time, I had just put it up. There were many friends I knew or had heard of, but others whom he had only known around Villanova. He had not inherited his father's skill at carpentry nor his love for gardening, but he had inherited his geniality, warmth, love for laughter, and ability to make people like him.

Made in the USA
Columbia, SC
26 May 2024

36099639R00128